Magic Moments:

four seasons on a Scottish hill farm

The author

'Tom Duncan' is the pen name used by Rog Wood for his perennially popular farming column in the *Sunday Post*. He has been a working farmer for nearly thirty years on his 700-acre sheep-and-cattle hill farm near Sanquhar in Dumfriesshire. He writes regularly for a wide range of newspapers including *The Scotsman*, *The Herald* and the *Yorkshire Post* and also contributes to many farming publications. In addition, Wood has worked for BBC Television on programmes such as *Landward* and *Countryfile*.

Magic Moments:

four seasons on a Scottish hill farm

Tom Duncan

Fort Publishing Ltd

First published in 2004 by Fort Publishing Ltd, 12 Robsland Avenue, Ayr, KA7 2RW

Reprinted 2004 (twice), 2006, 2007

Printed by Bell and Bain, Glasgow

Graphic design by Mark Blackadder

Typeset by S. Fairgrieve (0131-658-1763)

ISBN 10: 0-9544461-8-6
ISBN 13: 978-0-9544461-8-5

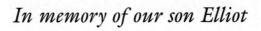

In memory of our son Elliot

Contents

SUMMER

1

Getting started

As with our birth, with death we have no choice. Death is nature's way of making room for the next generation and with all life it's the next generation that is more important.

Genetic progress is the key to nature's success. Over the years farmers have bred cattle and sheep that are bigger and meatier. They have grown better crops that yield more grain or oil. It's the same with people. We gradually change or evolve over the generations, but one thing never changes: we all wish our children to have good prospects in the future.

For a farmer, that means handing on the farm in good heart and with sound finances to his son. Farming is perhaps unique in the way generation after generation follow in their father's footsteps.

Europe is a mass of small farms because of the Napoleonic code of inheritance that gave children equal rights. As each generation died the children divided the land up equally. End result is thousands of non-viable, part-time farms. In Scotland we're more fortunate as our system favoured the eldest son. That is why our farms are so much bigger. They were passed on intact.

Though it's a good way of preserving big farms, it's not altogether fair on the rest of the family. Sisters and younger brothers often get a raw deal. It's a bit like a young cuckoo chick that has to push all the others out of the nest to be sure it survives.

Mind you, it's hard to see an alternative.

My own father's farm and livestock were worth about £1 million. As we never got on, he left everything to my younger brother. Had he divided the farm between my two sisters, my younger brother and me, it would have had to be sold. There was no way that my brother could have safely borrowed £750,000 to give us our shares. Worse, he would have ended up without a farm and livelihood. Instead, he was given the chance to carry on farming, my sisters and I are no worse off and my father's life work is kept intact.

My brother isn't really any better off than the rest of us. The farm and stock aren't spending money, but precious assets to be nurtured and passed onto the next generation. As my father said to me before he died, 'You will find that you can't be fair in farming.'

I well remember a family friend suggesting to my father that my brother might decide to spend the capital rather than farm with it. 'I hope he gets as much pleasure out of spending it, as I got out of making it', was my father's reply.

Fortunately I had managed to start farming on my own long before he died. My father and I were too alike for our own good and we parted company when I was in my early twenties.

I remember being at a market one day and admiring an out-standing pen of cattle. I turned to a friend and remarked that the seller was a good farmer who never sold bad stock. To which my friend quipped the old adage, 'Aye, but you seldom see a good farmer in a bad farm.'

In other words, perhaps it's the quality of the land that gives impressive yields and growth rates rather than outstanding ability to farm. Then again, maybe good farmers instinctively steer clear of bad farms and seek out good ones. Easier said than done!

When my father was thinking of buying his farm he asked the old farmer who was selling it what kind of harvests he could expect. 'They're usually fairly good although a bad one can set you back five or six ewes', he replied. That puzzled my father, so later on in the afternoon he asked the old man what he had meant. It turned out that the old farmer had been in the habit of hiring tramps to help with the harvest and, as well as sleeping in the bothies, they were also given free meals as part of the deal. Being a canny farmer, he fed them mutton from old ewes that were slaughtered on the farm, so if the harvest was prolonged by wet weather they could end up eating half a dozen!

At one time there were large numbers of travelling folk, mostly Irish, who moved through Scotland following seasonal farm work. There is a bridge across a burn, at the end of my farm road, that has one of its arches on dry land. Travelling folk regularly slept under that arch, and there is still an old brass bed under it that testifies it was once used as free, overnight accommodation.

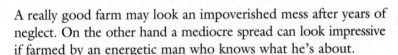

A really good farm may look an impoverished mess after years of neglect. On the other hand a mediocre spread can look impressive if farmed by an energetic man who knows what he's about.

However, in the absence of intimate local knowledge, there are telltale signs of a farm's real potential if you know what to look for.

Obviously, those that have been in the same family for generations are to be preferred to those that change hands regularly. Generally, good farms tend to have substantial farmhouses. After all, it took big profits to build, maintain and run them.

A quick glance at the farm buildings is another good indicator. But don't fall into the trap of looking at buildings erected in the last thirty years with government or European grants.

Instead turn your eyes to the traditional stone-steadings constructed in the nineteenth century.

In those days most of Scotland's farmers were tenants. Canny lairds seldom built large steadings on farms that couldn't pay rents to justify the expenditure. So, while a farm may now be covered in rough grasses, rushes and weeds, if it has a large stone barn and lots of stabling for Clydesdales, that's a sure sign it was once highly productive.

Even the name of the farm tells a lot about its character. Feu duties were paid in Scots merks based on farm production. So a farm called Merkland may not have been as good as Fourmerkland. Some farms often incorporate the title 'home farm'. That was often the best farm on the estate, farmed by the laird. Another good name to look out for is Sunnyside.

Snag with farming, as with all businesses, is that averages hide a wide range of performances. At times when the average farmer is losing money, the top 15 percent are still making good profits. And don't forget the bottom 25 per cent, who are losing money so fast they will soon be out of business. Average farmers survive by working hard and not spending money.

Top farmers with good profits have enough surplus cash to reinvest in their farms. That way they always have the best equipment, livestock or buildings. As with all walks of life the most efficient keep getting bigger and better.

Something like a fifth of Britain's farms account for 80 per cent of output. In other words, 80 per cent of us farming smaller spreads only produce 20 per cent. It's very humbling to be average!

Top farmers don't work any harder and they are not necessarily cleverer. Their secret is attention to detail. By constantly checking their crops for weeds and diseases, or tending to every whim of their livestock, they produce that little bit extra.

They are just as canny with their chequebook, but always use inputs like sprays and fertilisers more efficiently. There is seldom any waste on a top farm. They always manage to drive a harder bargain when buying or selling. Particularly when selling. That's because top farmers always produce top quality and that sells at a premium.

Remarkably, top farmers find recessions are opportunities to expand. That is often when they go on the expansion trail to become even bigger and more efficient. In the recession of the 1920s many hard-up Scottish farmers moved south and took over bankrupt English farms that were offered rent-free by landlords desperate for tenants. Like all top farmers, they went on to prosper in adversity.

Desperately short of money I had to find a farm to rent to get started. Tenancies are rarely offered on the open market so there was a lot of interest when mine was advertised. It was carrying 40 beef cows and 380 ewes but had the potential to carry a lot more and was an ideal size for a young couple looking for their first spread. Land has always been very expensive relative to farming profits and renting is the best option for those short of capital. At least forty prospective tenants viewed my farm and there were more than twenty offers.

When a farm is offered for let, the prospective tenants tender an annual rent. The offer is supported by budgets to show the tenant is capable of paying that rent and making a profit. References have also to be supplied and I remember when my father was looking for a second farm to rent, he wrote on his application that his farm was his reference and that it was open to inspection at any time. He was very proud of his ability as a farmer!

The factor or agent then draws up a short list of potential tenants with proven ability and offering a high rent. Sometimes it's simply a matter of who knows you, rather than who you know!

Finally he satisfies himself that the chosen person has the capital to stock the farm without borrowing too much. The last thing the laird wants is a bankrupt tenant who can't pay his rent.

There lies the snag. Machinery and livestock are expensive and it takes a lot of money to get a farm up and running. Tenancies in those days had little or no security. After an initial five to ten year period the laird had the right to evict the tenant. You would have thought that few people were prepared to invest a lot of money in an uncertain future. You would have thought that few would be mad enough to tie up a small fortune for the privilege of working long hard hours for little reward.

I am reminded of a cartoon I once saw, where two farmers

were leaning on a gate watching a tramp walk down a country road. One farmer turns to the other and says, 'he used to be a farmer but now he doesn't owe a penny to anyone'. There is more to life than money!

Surprisingly there were many disappointed hopefuls. The outgoing tenant, who had been born on the farm, was seventy-two-years old and had allowed the farm to become badly run down. I suspect that my laird selected me as his new tenant reckoning that youthful enthusiasm would soon get the farm back in good heart. So in May 1976 I found myself tenant of a 700-acre rundown hill farm.

Land is a finite resource, basically eternal and always patient. While it may be nice to own land, the real pleasure comes from controlling and managing it. As a tenant I reap the rewards of farming land as well as enjoying being its custodian. My objective is to leave my farm in better shape than when I first came to it. As man belongs to the earth, dust to dust, it follows that land cannot belong to man.

What we Scottish farmers refer to as the 'May term' officially falls on Whit or 15 May, and the 'November term' falls on Martinmas or 11 November. Nowadays the twenty-eighth of both those months are regarded as the 'term' dates. Both are important dates in the farming calendar and they are when farm tenancies and staff contracts are traditionally started or ended. They are also popular dates for entry to a farm that has been sold.

Two or three weeks before the term there is often a host of farm sales. They are widely advertised in the agricultural press with a full inventory of all that's to be put under the hammer. Friends come from far and wide to give the outgoing farmer or his widow a helping hand. And those extra bids can fairly push up the size of the nest egg at the day's end.

Farm sales tend to be social occasions as well as business outings and give everyone the chance to examine the farm and its buildings intimately. They are quite literally a field day for Nosey Parkers.

They mostly start about 10 a.m. when, after following a series of wee hand-painted signs round a labyrinth of back roads, you are eventually guided into the car park, which is usually a field. The secret is to park on top of a knowe near the gate. If it rains the field quickly turns to glaur and trying to free a car stuck up to its axles isn't my idea of fun!

So on a bright day back in May 1976, at 10.30 a.m. prompt, the auctioneer started the sale for the outgoing tenant on the farm I was going to take over. Standing on a trailer he took bids from the gathered crowd as the various items were held aloft.

First to be sold were the small tools that had been laid out for inspection in a cattle shed. Picks, shovels, brushes, hoes and hammers gave way to halters, hand shears, electric shears and dosing guns. Then came the turn of socket sets, angle grinders, hydraulic jacks, spanners, welders and the like. There were also filing cabinets, ropes, a sledge, spare parts and lubricants.

Then there was the junk. Broken graips, frayed ropes, half-used medicine containers with labels missing, buckets of bent nails, boxes of rusted nuts and bolts. A lifetime's bits and pieces accumulated in a cluttered farm workshop. The attraction was that many lots sold for a couple of pounds. Nostalgic items like cartwheels, horse brass and oil lamps were snapped up.

Many was the time I saw the bemused auctioneer hold up an unknown tool from a bygone era to be quipped at by some old worthy, 'Aye, laddie, ye'll no' ken whit that's for!'

By noon the auctioneer had emptied that shed and was ready to tackle the implements laid out in a nearby field. While he was selling the rows of machinery, another auctioneer was selling unwanted household effects.

The old farmer and his wife were retiring to a smaller house and wanted to get rid of surplus furniture and the like. Dining tables, chairs, riding boots, cutlery, an accordion, wireless, dinner services and much more were all sold to local bargain-hunters.

My wife and I missed all that as we were keeping an eye on the main field to try and buy badly needed equipment. I stayed my hand and bought nothing as rows of machinery ranging from antique turnip cutters, gates, mowers, ploughs and trailers to tractors and a battered old pickup came under the hammer.

Finally everyone moved back to the farmyard to watch the cattle sold through a makeshift auction ring.

I returned the next day to conclude some business with the old tenant and was struck by the eerie silence that had fallen on that empty farm. It was waiting patiently for me to take over so that it would once again become a lived-in, lively place.

2

Shear magic

That first summer was a hectic time. My main priority was to get the farm stockproof because I believe that a farmer's job is to look after his animals and not waste his time looking for them.

I managed to hire a good fencing contractor who set about renewing the fences round the hayfields to prevent hordes of marauding sheep from eating them bare. Elsewhere a squad of dykers was busy rebuilding drystane dykes. I spent a lot of my time patching holes in fences, making temporary gates out of second-hand timber or erecting temporary fences to block gaps of fallen drystane dykes.

At that time, the government paid a grant of 50 per cent of the cost of rebuilding so I took advantage of the scheme. It took many years, a lot of hard work and a lot of money to pay the wages of the highly skilled drystane dykers, but it was worth it.

Dykes are vitally important on my type of farm. They form an impenetrable field boundary that prevents even the wiliest animal from escaping, unlike hedges and fences that can be crawled through.

Another great advantage of dykes is the shelter they offer. During a storm, the lee side of a dyke is as warm as a shed. Indeed many a lamb owes its life to the shelter of a dyke. In the same way, the shade of a dyke on a hot day gives relief to stock. Fences usually rot and fall apart every twenty-five years or so, but a properly built and well-maintained dyke will last two or three generations.

The biggest advantage of a dyke is that it should cost nothing to repair. Unlike a fence that needs expensive new wire or posts to repair, if a piece of dyke falls down, all the materials needed are lying there free of charge. It's simply a matter of taking off your jacket, rolling up your sleeves and getting on with it.

Mind you, dyking isn't that easy and professionals serve a long apprenticeship. Some amateurs rush the job and end up with very shaky looking rebuilds. I remember one dyker who worked with me for several years telling me about a time he visited a farm to price a job. As he got out of the car, a collie dog ran up to a dyke, stood on its hind legs and then leaned against the dyke with its forelegs before beginning to pee. So the dyker asked the farmer where his dog had learned to pee like that. 'It started that trick after it peed against a dyke that fell on top of him', he replied. 'Aye', said the dyker, 'his dykes were in an awfy state.'

It's a strange fact of life that just as stones appear to reproduce under ground, stones lying at a fallen-down dyke mysteriously disappear. Some get trampled out of sight in soft ground by cattle while bigger stones break up as a result of frost. End result was that the dykers were constantly pestering me for extra stones to help them maintain the height of the new dykes.

I carted many of them from heaps of abandoned stones gathered from cultivated fields. Larger ones, needed to strengthen the dyke, came from a heap of rubble created by old buildings I demolished.

One stone I handled had been a windowsill from a derelict cottage. On the underside was carved a heart surrounding the initials of two young lovers. I imagined them holding hands as they watched the sun set and wondered what became of them. Their tryst is now concealed in the new dyke, as it was the night they carved it under the window ledge.

Keeping sheep where they are supposed to be grazing is one of life's problems. I like the story about the wee boy at a village school that had a new teacher.

'Right', said the teacher, 'let's see what your arithmetic is like. If there are forty-two sheep in a field and twelve get out through a hole in the fence, how many are left?' Wee Johnny hardly had to think. 'None, miss', he said.

'Dear me, John', said the teacher, 'you don't know much about arithmetic.'

'Well, miss', said wee John, 'you dinna ken much about sheep.'

Any shepherd or farmer who has seen his flock disappear through a hole in quick succession would agree with that. It's another of life's mysteries that, if a lamb starts squeezing through a hole in a hedge when it's very small, it can still squeeze through the same hole when it's about five times the size. They always leave a piece of wool hanging from barbed wire or hawthorn that acts as a beacon to the rest of the flock, highlighting the newly-discovered escape route.

Young lambs love to crawl under gates. Part of the spring ritual is to waste valuable time catching sprightly lambs and then returning them to their anxious mothers. Such lambs grow up to be ewes that think they are limbo dancers and prove it by the way they can sashay under the bottom wire on a fence or gate.

Worst of all are the jumpers and there are some nimble-footed brutes that can clear a six-foot dyke in one bound. In those early years I had some extremely athletic ewes that had learned their skill as lambs clambering over the broken-down dykes.

Snag with jumpers is that others see them doing it and attempt the same trick. Those that can't jump properly end up knocking off top stones and before you know it there's another hole in the dyke.

Straying sheep are a real nuisance. Apart from the time wasted looking for them, there's also the ill will that is created when a neighbour's fields or crops are grazed by stray sheep.

I well remember a group of hill sheep that persistently jumped over the boundary, or 'march' dyke as we call it, to graze my neighbour's fields. His wife, Moaning Minnie as we called her, could be quite curt and used to telephone me with the following message.

'A, your sheep are in my fields. B, you will take them away immediately and, C, you will make sure they don't return.'

Not wishing to fall out with her I used to drop everything and head off with the dogs to fetch those sheep back. Then I would rebuild the patch of dyke they had jumped over. Invariably there would be a phone call the next day with what I called the ABC message informing me that those pesky sheep were back in her fields again. I had dozens of those phone calls.

We eventually stopped that by rebuilding that dyke and running a strand of barbed wire nailed to fence posts in such a way as to deter sheep from jumping.

One day I spotted that a bunch of my neighbour's sheep had jumped over the march and were grazing my hill. I immediately set off for home at a brisk pace to inform Moaning Minnie.

When she answered the phone I told her in no uncertain terms that 'A, her sheep were on my hill, that B, she should remove them immediately and that C, she should make sure they didn't return again.'

You can imagine my disappointment when she replied that she was far too busy for that kind of nonsense and hung up the phone.

Sheep are cunning creatures, the Houdinis of farm animals, constantly looking for ways into the next field where the grass is always greener. A more sinister side is that stray sheep can lead to deaths.

When we count our sheep at feeding time, we assume if the count is correct that all is OK. But a stray among the bunch could have made the numbers add up and concealed the fact there's another ewe ill somewhere.

At lambing time, sheep are constantly being moved from one

field to another. With over a thousand ewes, lambs and other sheep to keep track of, it's easy to make a mistake with the 'counts' that I pencil in my little pocketbook.

I once remember a ewe that had strayed and become unaccounted for. She had wandered far and wide before settling near a railway line to graze the embankment. For afters, she jumped into a pensioner's garden to nibble herbs and flowers.

Frustrated at the damage being done to her garden, the woman phoned her son who farms nearby. He recognised the sheep as mine and decided to catch and return the ewe and her lambs to me.

His mother had told him the ewe always ran under a railway bridge when making her escape from the garden. So he set a trap by sealing the other side of the bridge with a gate. Sure enough, the ewe ran under the bridge and was caught. Next problem was catching the lambs that had escaped at the last minute. Once again he set a trap by tying the ewe to the gate so that the lambs would run in to join their mum.

Just as they were about to go under the bridge into the makeshift pen, they were startled by a rabbit and ran up the embankment onto the line, straight into the path of an oncoming train. How those two lambs escaped being crushed to death is a mystery but, after the train had passed, they were standing safe and sound in the middle of the track. That experience taught the blighters that it's safer to stay at home!

I no longer have a problem with straying sheep now that my dykes and fences are in first-class order. The big secret with straying sheep is to catch them as soon as they start. If you don't, they will end up teaching the rest of the flock how it's done. Having caught them, I always clearly mark them with a colour aerosol spray and transfer them to Colditz. That's the name I have given to a field that's totally escape proof. There they stay until the next time sheep are going to market when they are sold.

Over the years I have wasted countless hours looking for strays.

As a result I have learned to be ruthless on wayward nomads. Their first mistake is their last and they are always sold.

Time flies when you are busy and all too soon we were well into June and it was time to start shearing the sheep.

During winter, the poor diet of sheep stops their fleece growing and a weak point develops in the wool fibres. By the end of May there is plenty of lush grass and they start to grow their new fleece for next winter. A gap between last year's fleece and this year's, called the rise, develops as the sheep prepare to cast their old fleece. Shearing or clipping sheep can start when the rise is about an inch, as that's enough room for the shearer to comfortably work his shears between the sheep's body and the old fleece. Waiting for that vital rise can be a frustrating time.

Some ewes run about with parts of their fleece hanging off, while others have completely lost theirs. Everywhere there are small pickles of wool lying about, making fields look untidy. Worse still, sheep get itchy at that time of year. In warm showery weather especially, they love to roll over onto their itchy backs for a good rub on the ground.

Unfortunately, because of their shape and the weight of a wet fleece, they sometimes can't roll back over to get to their feet again, and may die as a result. You see, a couped sheep can't ruminate properly and that leads to a build up of gas in their stomachs that can soon be fatal. They may look ridiculous lying on their backs with four feet pawing at the sky but it's a serious predicament.

Fortunately the cure is simply a matter of rolling them back over and steadying them until they regain their balance. Checking the flock twice or thrice a day is time consuming and time was something I was desperately short of. Some farmers leave an old trailer in the field or nail a wooden crossbar between two posts so that itchy ewes can rub their backs whilst standing, but I reckon the surest way to deal with the problem is to clip them as soon as possible.

I used to clip the sheep myself when I was younger, but was never particularly good at it. A skilled shearer can easily manage 300 sheep a day whilst my best tally was 120 after a long, weary struggle. That was when I decided it was better to hire-in shearers and concentrate on making sure those shearers had a constant supply of sheep in the pens.

Top shearers are super athletes. They need the eye and skill of a marksman and the stamina of a marathon runner. Working bent over double and shearing a sheep weighing upwards of seventy kilos is backbreaking, tough work. Experts make it look easy, but I can tell you from experience that sheep really struggle if they aren't properly held.

As I said I used to clip my own sheep but, to do that, I needed casual workers to help with catching the sheep for me as well as to roll the fleeces and pack them into the wool sacks or sheets as we call them.

Fortunately I enlisted the aid of two good workers, in Cha and Big Tam. Cha is a near neighbour in a smaller farm where extra income is always welcome. He is a small, wiry man with an attitude problem when it comes to rules and regulations, and I well recall a tale that illustrates that point.

Legislation was introduced back in 1989 as a result of the food scare that resulted from Edwina Currie's outburst on the level of salmonella infection in eggs. Anyone with more than twenty-five hens had to take regular samples that were sent to a veterinary investigation officer for tests. The hens were destroyed if salmonella was detected. That had happened to a flock of hens kept by some nuns that made headline news.

Due to government cutbacks, there wasn't enough money to pay independent scientists to collect samples, so it was left to the farmer. If you were a poultry farmer would you send off samples you knew contained salmonella, aware it would mean the slaughter of your hens? Not likely, and there were rumours in farming circles that large poultry-farmers were screening samples in their own small labs, and only sending those that tested free of salmonella.

The owners of smaller flocks were putting the swabs in a microwave to kill the salmonella bacteria before sending them away, so they too would show up as negative. Daftest of all, it was perfectly legal to import foreign, untested eggs.

Cha kept about seventy free-range hens as a profitable little sideline, so I asked him about the proposed legislation. With his usual bluntness he replied, 'how can they ask a man to send honest samples if it runs the risk of losing his livelihood? 'In fact', he added with a wry smile, 'only nuns would send honest samples!'

I then asked him how he was going to get round the legislation. 'It doesn't affect me', he declared. 'I only have twenty-four hens. My wife owns another twenty-four, and my wee boy keeps twenty-two!'

He also has a wry sense of humour. On one occasion he went to the local ironmonger to buy a pound of nails. 'How long do you want them?' asked the shop assistant. 'I had hoped you would let me keep them', Cha cheekily replied.

Despite his carefree manner he is a hard worker and very knowledgeable with sheep as well as a highly skilled shearer. Big Tam on the other hand was a teacher who had taken early retirement. He is the exact opposite of Cha and has a schoolteacher's studied approach to everything he undertakes. He enjoys working outdoors on a farm and would probably offer his services free of charge.

So, in the middle of June, the three of us started to clip the ewe hogs, tups and any barren ewes that weren't rearing lambs.

Those ewes that are suckling young lambs aren't clipped till July. It is possible to clip them earlier, but there's the risk of sheep catching a chill if the weather turns cold and wet.

That's not necessarily serious for the ewe, but such a setback would cut her milk production. Lambs having their growth checked for want of milk is no way to make a profit from sheep.

It's important to shear sheep when they are dry because damp wool doesn't store well. We used to clip outdoors in pens that had no roof so it was important to pick a day that promised to stay dry. There's nothing worse than having to return unclipped sheep to their field because it has started to rain.

Cha had predicted that day was going to be glorious. He's a great one for relying on nature to forecast the weather and thinks little of weather experts on television.

The previous evening when we were laying our plans he had pointed to the glorious red sky. 'Bound to be good tomorrow', he said. I told him he was havering and, although a red sky in the morning never failed to be a sign of a wet day, a red sky at night was no sure guide.

He agreed with that, but pointed to the swallows. 'When they fly high like that for insects, it's a sign of high pressure', he insisted.

Next morning there was heavy dew. We couldn't get the sheep into the pens to clip them without soaking their wool on the long dew-laden grass. As we sat and patiently waited for it to lift, Cha explained that heavy dew was also a sign of a good day. Sure enough, the day was glorious and we had a full day's clipping. With more than half of them done, Cha confidently predicted the next day would also be a scorcher. Again he used the high-flying swallows and the red sky to back up his forecast.

Next morning I was out at 6.30 a.m. in beautiful bright sunshine. Gathering the sheep on the hill that morning for the day's clipping was as pleasant a task as you could find. But Cha had changed his mind from the day before. 'Too bright too early', he announced. 'Nae dew is a bad sign and the wind's out of the wrong direction', he added. By lunchtime the sky had darkened and the swallows were swooping low.

Panic was setting in as we frantically tried to finish clipping that bunch of sheep before the rain came on. Big Tam, struggling to keep up with rolling the fleeces, announced we'd have to stop clipping in five minutes.

Cha agreed. 'When you can't see yon hill', he declared, 'the rain's not far off.' Tam snorted that the spots of rain he could feel on his bald patch were a surer sign. Half an hour later we were sitting round the kitchen table having a cup of tea watching the rain bouncing off puddles in the yard.

Wool used to pay the rent on a hill farm like mine. Gradually over the years its value has declined until in recent years it barely covers the cost of shearing. British wool is coarser than fine wool from merinos that are kept in hot dry countries like Spain, Australia and South Africa. Three-quarters of British wool, is made into carpets and because it is so bulky it gives a carpet a luxurious feel. But I wasn't concerned about the value of my wool or its ultimate use. I had to finish shearing so I could get on with the rest of the summer work.

Fortunately the weather cleared again and we got those sheep back into the pens a few days later. There was a hiccup when Cha tried to knock-off wool that was sticking to a brush and managed to break the shaft. That led to Tam giving Cha a lecture on taking care with things. Cha decided to get his own back and quietly slipped Tam's bonnet among the fleeces in one of the wool sheets. At the end of the day, when Tam was looking for his bonnet, Cha delivered a long-winded lecture on taking care of things. It was over a month before Tam was reunited with his bonnet after I made a special request for the wool graders at the depot to keep an eye out for it.

3

Cha and the tar boys

Short of capital, I couldn't afford extra cows to expand the herd so I bought a lot of young heifer calves to rear that summer.

They were thirty Aberdeen-Angus-cross-Friesian heifer-calves that I hoped would expand my herd in the future. Those bonnie black calves looked a picture as the dealer unloaded them off his lorry and I was very proud of them until later that afternoon when my wife and I tried to feed them. What a fiasco!

The idea was to get them to drink milk out of a bucket but most of them had other ideas. Some had been suckling old nurse cows whilst others were used to artificial milk from a rubber teat. Only a handful knew how to drink from a bucket. We would mix milk powder with warm water and put a couple of pints into a small bucket. Then you cornered a calf, restrained it and, having put your hand into the milk, encouraged it to suckle your fingers. Next stage was gently lowering your hand into the milk so that the calf would suck milk through your fingers. Finally you eased your fingers out of its mouth as it suckled, leaving it drinking. As with many farm jobs the theory is simpler than the practice.

Just as you lowered its head into the bucket it would flick it into the air drenching you with milk. Fortunately hunger is a good tutor and most calves mastered the art of drinking from a bucket within a few days. Sadly those that didn't learn quickly got a reprieve as one of the biggest disasters of my farming career started to unfold.

My cows had only been on their new farm a few weeks when I moved them from the fields to the hill for the summer. That hill was riddled with ticks that attacked those cows with a vengeance. Ticks transmit a whole range of diseases and that summer they infected my cows with tick fever, a disease for which they had no immunity, as they had never grazed tick-infested land before. One of the symptoms of tick fever is that the cows run a high temperature.

I had noticed some of the cows going off colour, but they seemed to recover fairly quickly. About a week later they started to abort dead calves. Nowadays my herd calves in the spring but in those days most of them were due to calve in the autumn.

Each morning for about a week, I would have to bring one or two aborted cows into the byre to be tied by the neck by a chain.

Normally when a cow has a dead calf you skin it and drape the skin over the calf you intend to foster on. The cow smells the skin of her dead calf and assumes the foster calf is hers. But those aborted calves were so small their skins would never fit over a healthy calf. So I had to encourage those cows to adopt a calf by standing patiently with them three times a day to make sure they let it suckle without kicking it. It was an immense amount of extra work and not always successful. Some cows stubbornly refused to accept their calves for several weeks and one had to be brought into the byre morning and night for the rest of the summer.

All too soon it was July and the ewes that were suckling lambs had to be clipped and I also needed to start making hay. Fortunately the summers of 1976 and 1977 were scorchers although I couldn't predict that and had to assume that every dry day was precious. The clipping was easily finished and it was grand to send the wool away and get my first cheque.

It's amazing how events conspire to hold you back when you are really busy. One of my biggest problems in those early years was dealing with the hordes of sales reps that used to call unannounced at the farm. Nowadays most of us do our business by phone or arrange a specific time for a rep to call. Most of our suppliers prefer it that way, rather than send reps cold-calling around the countryside. Some of them were so persistent that you had to be rude to get rid of them.

Cha reckoned that he was a leading authority on rep prevention and evasion. According to him, the first golden rule is that prevention is better than cure. To that end farm roads should be kept rough and muddy, and interspersed with plenty of gates, ropes and other necessary paraphernalia for herding cows. 'Most reps hate the thought of getting out of their snug cars on a wet day to open gates, particularly when their immaculately polished shoes get covered in muck,' he stressed. 'Should they succeed in arriving at the steading you must make yourself scarce,' he added.

Another good line of defence he employed was that of disguise. He reckoned that was a particularly satisfying ploy that worked best on the more arrogant and inexperienced reps. He recounted the tale of a suave young rep that had called at his farm and asked if the boss was about. Cha had then acted like an illiterate peasant and replied that the boss was a waster and probably in the pub with his fancy woman.

Perhaps the worst kind to shake off were the 'tar boys'. They used to land in the yard at lunchtime with an aged Mercedes, smoking a cigar and speaking with an Irish or Liverpudlian accent. They would tell you that they had a contract on the motorway, but that due to bad weather or a breakdown they had a couple of loads of tarmac to spare and wondered if you would like them cheap.

That had also happened to Cha who had accepted the offer on condition that his cheque wasn't presented at the bank for a couple of weeks. That immediately brought forth a suspicious enquiry as to why the cheque needed to lie for two weeks. Cha had told him in confidence that the bank had stopped honouring his cheques, but that he had a good accountant who would sort it all out in a couple of weeks. 'Being a chancer, the thought of dealing with another chancer sent him running a mile,' laughed Cha.

Scotland's cattle used to winter on a diet of hay, straw and chopped Swedes – or neeps as we call them – supplemented with a cereal-based concentrate. That was fine in the days when there was a large farm workforce. As the number of farm workers declined so did the acreage of neeps.

Neeps – like their close cousin oilseed rape, the crop with bright yellow flowers that produces small dark seeds that are crushed to extract cooking-oil – are ideally suited to our Scottish climate. They grow well in our long summer days and our cooler temperatures mean they aren't attacked by disease-bearing pests, as happens down south.

Neeps were generally sown on land that had grown cereals the previous year. After harvest, in late autumn, the stubble would have had liberal amounts of muck from the midden spread on it before being ploughed down for the winter. It was worked into a fine tilth in the spring, formed into drills and then the tiny turnip seeds were sown in May. The real work started shortly after the rows of seedlings started to appear.

Squads of folk ranging from the regular workforce to pensioners, kids and casual workers were drafted in to thin those young neep plants with hoes. The squad would work their way up the drills in a diagonal line with the most skilled in the lead and the slowest at the rear. Idea is to push out surplus young neep plants with the hoe, leaving selected individual plants spaced a hoe-width apart. Then you had to scrape the weeds off the side of the drill. Done properly in fine dry weather you ended up with a weed-free field of regularly spaced neeps. But it was monotonous, hard, backbreaking work. The only relief was the crack from the rest of the squad when we stopped for a piece break.

I have many happy memories of sitting in the warm sunshine with my flask and pieces. Time was as precious then as now. Going back to the house for a tea break wasted a good twenty minutes, so we always carried a piece bag. Simple but delicious pieces they were. Cheese sandwiches with homemade chutney. Pieces of home baking like shortbread or fruitcake washed down with a flask of sugary tea.

During hot spells, we carried bottles of cold tea or mealy water made by steeping oatmeal overnight. While that may sound disgusting to those reared on Irn Bru or Coke it was truly refreshing, particularly when left in a burn to chill.

Many are the times I've sat munching away listening to the grown-ups. Local gossip, yarns, jokes or just a general discussion on the day's work. Then, just as we were getting settled, someone would flick the tea leaves out of his cup and announce, 'this shan't get the work done.' Piece time used to have a magic all of its own and was a welcome break in a hard, monotonous day's work. There was also the smell of tobacco as the pipes were kindled.

But times change. Workers were laid off and most of us now work by ourselves. Land Rovers, pick-ups and quad bikes have become commonplace, allowing us the luxury of nipping back to the house.

Worse, my anxious wife, ever mindful of my middle-age spread, started to lay out crisp-bread spread with cottage cheese, apples or yoghurt. Soon I learned not to bother with tea breaks at all. Farming is too rushed nowadays. It was grand to sit there savouring a piece of apple tart and watching the world go by, enjoying the smells of the fields and hills and the sounds of wildlife. It's maybe just as well I don't carry a piece bag nowadays as I would get nothing done.

Those neep drills had to be regularly scarified during the

summer. That involved driving a tractor slowly up the drills with a mechanical hoe drawn behind. Everything that was ever done to neeps during the summer required dry weather.

Then followed the autumn ritual of lifting the neeps by hand and cutting off the roots and the thick neck with leaves, or shaws as we call them, with a heavy sickle-type, shawing knife. Neeps were thrown into one row ready to be carted to the pit where they were to be stored for the winter, whilst the green shaws were cast into a separate row to be carted daily as a fresh, succulent feed for the beasts.

Shawing neeps is a miserable, backbreaking job. Frosty shaws in the morning or the recently thawed water on them left your hands numb and eventually lead to those nasty open sores called gegs.

Every morning, for the rest of the winter, neeps had to be carted from their straw-covered pit to be chopped into pieces and then carted again to the beasts. No wonder few can be bothered to grow neeps today! The only good thing about neeps was that cattle enjoyed them and thrived.

I'll never forget the time an agricultural adviser was explaining to my father that growing swedes was labour intensive and not an efficient way of feeding cattle. 'They're 90 per cent water', he added, by way of driving his point home. 'Aye', replied my father, 'But it's awfy good water.'

Although I have grown neeps in the past, they were only for winter grazing to fatten lambs and always precision sown. That's a modern technique involving sprays that prevent weeds from germinating and specialist equipment that sows individual seeds on a level surface, at the correct distance apart. There is no way I am prepared to go back to the old ways of growing them.

'Making hay while the sun shines', is a lot easier said than done. If only we could predict when the sun is going to stay around long enough! I have often let the first couple of days of fine weather slip by before I was sure that it was the start of a settled spell. The penalty for such caution is that it invariably rains a day or two before you manage to get the hay dry enough to bale.

I must confess to having been the unluckiest haymaker of all time. Even in the driest summer I had the uncanny knack of attempting to make mine in the only wet or humid spell. Many is the year I have hesitated to mow, whilst all around were steadily progressing the season's work.

Within a couple of days of being convinced that the weather was settled and making a start, the heavens would open.

Then came the ritual of spreading out wet hay to dry a couple of times, followed by gathering the stuff back into neat rows ready for the baler, followed by a torrential downpour. It's frustrating watching a heavy downpour undo all your work. Now I know what my wife goes through, drying washing on a showery day. Over a few weeks, that sequence eventually makes the crop change colour from lush green to an unappetising greyish black.

A hay crop that has been kicked about for several weeks loses a lot of leaf and yields half the number of bales.

Badly weathered hay has virtually no feed value and merely fills hungry bellies. It's almost as bad as mouldy hay that was baled too soon. Hay that isn't properly dried soon heats and goes mouldy. More good hay is wasted by baling a day too soon, than is ever wasted by bad weather.

But it takes nerves of steel to hold off from baling hay that is nearly ready, when the clouds are gathering at the end of a good spell.

Good hay is a tremendous feed. Silage may well have a better nutritional analysis, but it is cold, wet and has a strong acidic smell. Few animals can resist a bite of well-won meadow hay. There's nothing like it for stimulating the appetite of a sick animal in winter. Good hay has a unique, sweet, heady fragrance like a plate of mince and tatties after a foreign holiday. Irresistible!

Inventing the knotter was one of the big breakthroughs in agriculture. It's the mechanism that ties a knot in twine and it revolutionised farming, allowing us to mechanically tie up bunches of corn into sheaves and making harvesting easier.

Later, balers were invented that produced compact twenty-five kilo bales of fodder neatly held together by a couple of lengths of twine. That took a lot of backache out of haymaking, as it meant old hayforks could be thrown aside. Knotters-on balers and binders also gave farmers their greatest resource; hundreds of miles of baler twine.

Without twine, most farmers would be lost. We all carry a bunch of the stuff in our pockets or under the tractor seat.

When a sheep strays or is ill and needs to be brought in for treatment, we tie her to a fence post while we fetch the Land Rover or tractor. It can be used in a difficult lambing to help keep the wee lamb's head in its proper position during birth.

Elsewhere, twine can secure the skin on a calf that is being fostered. But its versatility in repairing things is phenomenal.

Gates are securely tied shut with twine when the latch or sneck is broken. Broken wooden gate-spars are permanently bound together by twine. Holes in a wire-net fence can be mended by forming a web with twine.

Leaking water pipes won't leak quite as badly if a piece of polythene or cloth is wrapped round and then securely bound with twine. All kinds of machinery repairs can be temporarily effected with twine and a little ingenuity. It's amazing how some of those temporary repairs last for years! Best use is for making temporary cattle or sheep pens. A few fence posts, a stack of pallets and some old gates can be transformed into useful pens if properly tied with twine.

Key to success lies in correct handling of the twine. It must always be cut next to the knot, as there's nothing worse than a length of twine with a knot halfway along.

After cutting the bales, all the twine should be gathered up and hung by the knots in big bunches, otherwise it becomes a tangled mass of rubbish. It should never be left lying about, as modern polypropylene twine is virtually indestructible. Mixed with bedding straw it ultimately clogs the muck spreader by wrapping around the chains and flails. It's only after you have spent a messy morning trying to cut it all off with a penknife that you realise how tough twine really is.

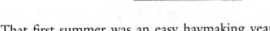

That first summer was an easy haymaking year and I had every nook and cranny filled with bales of hay that had never had a drop of rain on them. I stopped making hay a few years later and started making silage, as it's a surer way of securing winter rations in a typically wet Scottish summer.

Silage is simply pickled grass. Grass is consolidated in the silage pit to exclude any air. It's then sealed airtight by covering it with a plastic sheet weighted down by old tyres. In the absence of oxygen, anaerobic bacteria convert sugar in the grass to lactic acid. Eventually that process stops and the grass is preserved by the acid. If you don't keep the air out, the aerobic bacteria produce butyric acid that leads to smelly silage that cows don't like. So the secret is to fill the pit as quickly as possible and get it covered with the sheet.

It also helps to wilt the grass for about a day after cutting. Less water in the grass means less acid is needed to preserve it. And of course there are fewer problems with silage effluent. It's an obnoxious liquid that has a high biological oxygen demand (BOD). If it is allowed to seep into waterways, it uses up all the oxygen in the water and suffocates the fish. By law we have to collect silage effluent in sealed tanks and then spread it on fields well away from burns, rivers and lochs. So the less that's produced the better.

I started making silage in the early eighties with a set of unreliable second-hand equipment that seemed to be constantly in the workshop for repairs. Nowadays I hire in contractors who can do the entire job in just two days. Massive mowers cut the grass into big, dark-green swathes. Then tedders (spinning-disc rakes) shake out the grass to wilt in the sun. That's followed by a machine that gathers it back into rows for the harvester that lifts it, chops it and blows it into trailers.

The secret is to fill the pit as quickly as possible, roll it solid with tractors and seal it with plastic sheets. And that's one of the drawbacks of making silage. Those sheets have to be weighted down with hundreds of old tyres and throwing them onto the pit can be a very unpleasant, sweaty task. Invariably, waist-high nettles grow up through the tyres and, as you lift them, they flatten the nettles against your wrist and forearms leading to unpleasant nettle rashes.

Next snag is that the tyres have lain full of smelly stagnant water and as they land you often get splashed. And of course, stagnant water is an ideal breeding ground for midges. Silage pits are invariably sheeted over in the evening, unfortunately an ideal time for all those disturbed midges to take their revenge!

One of the sad aspects of making hay or silage is the amount of wildlife that is maimed or killed by fast-moving mowers. It's sickening to see birds like partridges and pheasants literally mowed down as they crouched, unseen, on their clutch of eggs.

I regularly inspect my fields in the run up to silage time so that I can decide the optimum time to start cutting. One night, as I left a field, I heard a squeaking noise behind me. One of my dogs had found a young hare, or leveret, hiding in the long grass.

Hares hide their three or four leverets in different places. Unlike rabbits, they're born with their eyes open and fully furred. This one was just a few days old and had been hidden in a thick patch of grass near the gate.

As we left it, none the worse for its fright, I couldn't help thinking how lucky it had been. The mother would return to suckle it, smell both my scent and that of the dog and shift her youngster to a new hideaway. That's just as well. A leveret as young as that wouldn't have got out of the way of the silage equipment and would probably been killed.

It's a pity animals can't understand that what looks like a safe haven can often be a death trap.

4

'You should never trust a bull'

It often seems to me that sheep have a death wish. Without a shepherd's constant care I am convinced they would have become extinct centuries ago.

Milk fevers, pneumonia, couping and drowning are just some of their favourite ways to end it all. On top of those, they have plenty others up their sleeve. Just when you're convinced you know every possible way for them to die, a sheep will prove you wrong and come up with a new method.

It makes no difference to a sheep whether it is summer or winter. Summer diseases tend to be different from winter ones, although external parasites feature all-year round.

Woolly sheep are constantly under attack from a host of creepy-crawlies. During the winter there are biting lice, keds and sheep-scab mites. They're extremely irritating and cause sheep to rub themselves against fence posts or to constantly nibble their itchy fleeces. The end result can be sorry-looking sheep with straggly broken fleeces.

In the spring there are ticks that jump onto sheep to suck their blood. That's not as painful as it sounds, but it spreads serious diseases such as tick-borne fever, border disease or louping-ill.

During the summer there are head flies that attack the skin at the base of the horn, creating nasty sores. Worst pests of all are greenbottles or blowfly. During spells of humid weather they lay their eggs on soiled parts of the fleece near the tail. Those eggs hatch into hundreds of maggots that can literally eat a sheep alive.

In the autumn, when the bracken starts to die back, I sometimes find skeletons of sheep that have died a painful death. Sheep logic is to hide from pain, making it impossible for me to find them as they cower beneath the waist-high canopy of bracken. Tragically that seals their fate, although those I do find are easily cured. It's simply a matter of clipping away wool from the infested area, scraping off the maggots with a penknife and then soaking the fleece with a solution of dip to prevent any more eggs from hatching.

Prevention is the key to success with sheep parasites and that's why we dip them. Sheep dip is simply a solution of pesticides and a good dip is one that contains the deadliest insecticide. Snag is, some are so deadly they kill other wildlife as well. Aldrin, DDT and deildrin were all good dips that were so deadly they had to be withdrawn.

DDT entered the food chain and caused infertility in birds of prey like sparrowhawks and kestrels. One of the more popular dips in use today is made from organophosphates. Developed from nerve gases, they are fairly reliable sheep dips, although they can cause human health problems if you don't wear specialist protective clothing.

Once I had the hay safely stored, I enlisted the assistance of Cha and Tam to dip the ewes and lambs.

Tam is a canny, big man. Unlike Cha, who loves to gossip, Tam prefers to keep his own counsel. I remember Cha was curious to know why Tam regularly took pills. 'I take a green pill, first thing in the morning, with a glass of water. Then I take a blue pill with a glass of water after lunch. Just before I go to bed I take a red pill with another glass of water', Tam solemnly advised him. 'What exactly is your problem?' asked Cha. 'My doctor reckons I don't drink enough water', Tam replied, leaving Cha no wiser.

Tam is one that likes to keep everything tidy. His garage is a sight to behold, with all the tools neatly hanging on their hooks, or carefully laid in their own place on the shelves. Gardening tools, like forks and spades, are washed, dried and then wiped with an oily rag before being put back where they belong.

There are rows of small tins containing every conceivable nut, bolt or washer. That impressive collection has been built up as a result of never throwing anything out. Redundant or irreparable electrical goods are carefully dismantled in order to salvage small components. 'You never know when they will come in handy', is a favourite quote of his.

I remember we were once repairing the sheep pens and Tam gave Cha a bent nail with the instruction that he was to fetch a dozen of that size from the workshop. When Cha dutifully returned with the appropriate nails, Tam enquired what he had done with the bent one. 'I threw it away' explained Cha. 'What a waste', replied Tam, 'it would have easily straightened.'

He is a leading authority on Robert Burns and often quotes lines from his poetry. Years of reciting poetry at Burns suppers has encouraged his thespian side and he is registered with an acting agency. From time to time, he acts as an extra in soaps and other television dramas. Apart from earning £50 a day, he reckons the real fun is mixing with different actors, and he is on first-name terms with some.

A friend of his works for the council and hands on his brightly coloured, fluorescent waterproofs. I remember Cha once poked fun at his gaudy outfit. 'It's amazing what some folk will wear, to get noticed', he quipped. 'O wad some Power the giftie gie us, to see oursels as ithers see us', Tam retorted with a quote from Burns.

It might come as a surprise, but not every sheep wants to jump into a long narrow tank full of water containing smelly chemicals. You know and I know it's in a good cause, but I have never yet managed to convince a sheep of that.

In my experience, they have two reactions. One is to dig their toes in and refuse to budge until pushed or hauled to the edge of the dipper and dropped in. Or they take a runner at it like an Olympic high diver or some athlete trying for a long-jump record.

They've no chance of clearing the dipper, which is about ten yards long. Mind you, I've given some particularly lively sheep nine out of ten for artistic impression before they belly flopped into the mixture. We had one wily old ewe that almost, but never quite, mastered the trick of jumping from side to side of the dipper, a bit like the wall of death. She always fell in eventually to be soaked like the rest, but every year she got a little bit further along.

Granted, it's not much fun for the sheep, and a hot, sweaty day trying to persuade sheep to go in, one way or another, isn't much fun for the farmer and his helpers either. Not for me pushing the sheep in and certainly not for Cha at dipper level making sure every sheep went completely under.

For the dip to do its job thoroughly, every bit of the sheep, from nose to tail, has to go under. Sheep should be in the dipper for at least a minute. That's not easy if a determined sheep is a good swimmer and wants out as fast as possible. It means that between pushing them right under and holding them back a bit, Cha got a right old soaking. Nowadays there's official safety gear that covers you from top to toe. Wearing wellingtons, waterproof trousers and tops, heavy-duty rubber gauntlets and a face shield make a warm day feel like being in a steamie, with all the steam coming from the wearer.

Not that my job was easier. Tam pushed the sheep forward to the pen where I caught them and put them into the dipper. As soon as the sheep spied that dipper, most of them turned about and headed for the back of the pen. So each one had to be manhandled.

Like most jobs there's a knack to it. The trick is to stand and encourage the sheep to run between the dipper and me. Just as it passes the mouth of the dipper, I catch it under the jaw with one hand, grip the fold of skin that's between the hindquarter and belly with my other hand and nudge it in with my knee. Properly done, that technique looks effortless, although it's not uncommon for the less experienced to slip and fall into the dipper as the wily ewe stands her ground.

Working hard all the time isn't good for anyone. I reckon that people who never need to take a break can't be working that hard in the first place. Truth to tell, without a wee break now and then I become scunnered and useless.

Like many other farmers I enjoy a day out at an agricultural show and there are always plenty to go to most weeks in the summer. They range from the four-day Royal Highland at Ingliston to a myriad of one-day local events.

Part of the fun is the drive to the show, as along the way you have the opportunity to inspect farming progress in other parts. Being a hill farmer I always make for the sheep-judging first to mix with old pals and catch up on the gossip.

You would hardly recognise us all in our Sunday best, although I have to say that the sheep usually put us to shame. Miss World isn't more pampered. White-faced sheep have had their faces washed before having chalk or talcum powder applied to make them look whiter. Blackface sheep have their horns sandpapered and oiled, their heads glistening with special dressings that the showmen use. And of course, every last one's fleece has been brushed and trimmed to make them look as big and meaty as possible.

It's all for a brief spell in the judging ring where a hundred other experienced judges watch the official judge take his pick. That's often followed by comments like, 'I wouldna hae picked that neb-nosed yowe', or 'why on earth does he fancy that yin? She stands like a cuddy!'

Showing is an important way of promoting a breeder's animals and comparing your stock with others. Many rams are sold in the autumn for top prices on the strength of their performance on the show circuit.

Many farmers, and their wives, play hard at showing livestock. Attention to detail is important and the way most animals are turned out is a credit to their stockmen. Dairy cattle are clipped, carefully washed and trained to walk and stand in the correct manner. An incredible amount of work goes in to parading animals at their peak. Many a fashion model reaches the catwalk with less preparation, but remember, the washing, blow-drying, brushing, combing and polishing of champion cattle is only the icing on the cake. The hard work has all been done back at the farm.

Many champions are homebred. A farmer has had to back his judgement in buying the best bull and choosing the right cows to breed from. Then he has to spot a potential winner as a young calf. He has got to get its feeding right and spend many an hour walking it around. Aye, and talking to it, because the best stock-men are on the same wavelength as their animals.

It's not daft to talk to animals. Good stockmen are often friendlier with their animals than with their fellow men.

I once worked on a pig farm when I was a student. The head pigman was always bad tempered with his workmates yet spoke kindly to his pigs. While we had no time for him and avoided him at all costs, I have to admit his pigs adored him.

Research confirms that animals thrive better if they have a good relationship with their stockman. Scientists have secretly watched stockmen at work and recorded how they interacted with their herds and flocks. Good stockmen talked with their animals. They also spent more time rubbing their noses or scratching their heads. In return, animals love to come up to a kindly stockman for some affection.

Contented cows let their milk down more easily, gave higher yields and suffered less from disease. Because good stockmen spent so much time with their charges, they noticed the little changes in behaviour that indicate when an animal is becoming poorly. They also spotted more animals in heat and so had better fertility results. Their animals were mated at peak times.

Bad stockmen were people who rushed about and never had time for their charges. They hit them with sticks or slapped them on the rump with their hand. Their animals were nervous and didn't thrive as well. Instead of talking quietly, they shouted commands in an aggressive manner.

Fortunately such behaviour is rare and most of us are kind to our animals; some eccentric stockmen even play music to them. It doesn't seem to matter if it is Beethoven or the Beatles, but a stockman whistling or singing a happy tune definitely makes animals more contented.

Pigs grow faster, hens lay more eggs and cows give more milk. Better still, happy and contented animals are easier to work with. They don't kick, bite or scratch. They don't charge about breaking gates or knocking people over. A quiet call soon has them all gathered round, eagerly waiting for a nose rub or titbit.

If you need to work with a sick animal, it's easier to slip a halter on a quiet one than one that's trying to escape out of fear.

Horsemen and dog handlers also share this special relationship with their charges to get the best out of them. Scientists have proved conclusively that it really does pay to talk to the animals.

After the livestock, there are the machinery lines to inspect where the latest equipment and techniques are on display. It's a rare chance to compare different makes of machinery and their prices.

It's also a chance to complain about faults. Parts that continually jam, weak points that break, inaccessible grease nipples or awkward guards. Often the manufacturer offers to modify your machine at a reduced price. It all depends on how hard you pester him and how many people are listening at the time.

After scrounging a sandwich lunch and a glass of beer from a supplier there is nothing I like better than to watch the events in the main ring. There are livestock parades, sheepdog trials, musical entertainment and showjumping to watch as well as the likes of the Royal Marines demonstrating their skills.

Just as I enjoy time off visiting an agricultural show so townsfolk enjoy spending time in the countryside. There's a nice wee pool on my hill at the junction where two burns meet. As it's beside a quiet country road, it's a picnic favourite.

Umpteen families have spread out a blanket on the short grass and had a picnic there. As mum and dad soak up the sun or read a paper, the bairns have a whale of a time paddling. Some build dams, splash each other or hunt baggy minnows with nets or jelly jars.

I like to see folk in the countryside enjoying all the beautiful sights, pleasures and pursuits it has to offer. It must be a grand outing for a family, used to the dismal surroundings of a city, to enjoy the freshness of the Scottish countryside.

Mind you, some of the townies give me a good laugh. Hikers with their big boots, rucksacks and survival packs setting off on adventurous hill climbs that shepherds have already done before breakfast. With sunburned shoulders and thighs they stride across hills in the midday sun.

Shepherds go to the hill at sunrise and walk in the cool of the morning. But for some reason, most townies prefer to do it the hard way. As Cha once remarked, 'either we're saft or they're saft in the heid.' To each his own. It's nice to see folk enjoying themselves, even if climbing steep braes in a heatwave isn't my idea of pleasure.

There are those picnickers who set up tables, deck chairs and barbecues to transform a lay-by into a three-star restaurant. Then, of course, there are those fancy caravans with central heating, showers, televisions, fridges and every luxurious fitting. Some townsfolk have more comforts and conveniences when they're camping than I have at home.

The Scottish Parliament gave everyone the right of access to the countryside. Foot-and-mouth demonstrated the importance of having visitors to the countryside, not least because they spend money in our local shops and hotels. It is important rural communities remain viable and keep country schools and post offices open. Visitors are also welcome, because they then develop a better understanding of country life.

I always believed that the public had a legitimate and historic right of access to all of Britain's countryside. Provided property, crops, livestock and privacy are respected, there was never any reasonable argument for denying access. The land belongs to the people.

They have defended it in times of war, they have subsidised it in times of peace and they should not be denied access to it by self-centred landowners. In the past, under tribal or clan systems, land was shared by all, for the benefit of the community as a whole. What is the point of farmers and landowners arguing that they are the custodians of the countryside if they will not allow the public access to it?

Having said that, the public has a duty of care. Disease can be spread among farm animals. The last outbreak of classical swine fever probably started with a discarded sandwich containing infected, imported meat that was eaten by a pig. Commonest complaint is litter. Bottles left lying eventually get broken. Clingfilm, crisp bags, newspapers and the like blow in the wind and end up hanging on fences and trees.

I remember one incident, when a five-month-old suckled calf got a rusty old can stuck on a hind foot. Cattle hooves are cloven; that is, they have two halves or clits. The calf had stood on a can left lying after a picnic and pushed a clit firmly into it. As that can crushed under the weight of the calf it became securely stuck.

Worse, the calf was in excruciating pain as the jagged edges formed by the can opener cut into the flesh at the head of the clit.

It was an unlikely accident. Walking that poor wee calf, along with its mother, the mile or so back to the farm steading wasn't easy. Frustrated and enraged by the pain, it kept charging off in all directions.

Eventually I got it into a shed and restrained it. A pair of tin shears soon cut the can free of the clit. The wound then had to be cleaned and dressed and the patient was injected with long-acting penicillin to prevent further infection. He soon mended but what made me angry was that the louts who left their litter are unlikely to mend their ways.

Then there are those who refuse to walk their dogs on a lead. Strange dogs upset sheep and can panic cattle into charging across their field and even jumping over a fence to escape.

The biggest problem is caused by not shutting gates properly. That's often due to ignorance rather than deliberate wilfulness. Town folk don't seem to realise it isn't enough simply to shut a gate. All the catches, chains and snecks must be securely in place as well. If not, cattle simply push the gate open when they rub their itchy necks or backsides against it.

There's nothing worse than different batches of livestock getting mixed up as a result of a gate not being securely shut.

Cattle can get hurt as they fight each other, maiden heifers can become pregnant too young, crops are eaten or trampled and disease spreads more easily. Then there's all the hassle of separating the animals that can take two or three people the best part of a day.

My main concern is that walkers could be hurt by cows protecting their newly born calves, or by charging bulls.

Most folk are quite rightly terrified of bulls. Even farmers like me, with a lifetime's experience, are wary of them.

Sadly, some farmers are injured or killed by a quiet beast they felt safe with rather than one they weren't sure of. Proving the old adage that 'you should never trust a bull'. Their mighty size and mighty bellow can be impressive but I assure you their strength is even more awesome than most of you can begin to imagine.

For years we were bothered by power cuts in our neighbourhood. Some occurred on wild, stormy nights but most were on calm summer evenings. Baffling!

It was only by chance that we discovered the problem was caused by a neighbour's bull with an itchy backside. Periodically the huge brute rubbed his rump against an electricity pole so vigorously that it shook the overhead power cables till they touched and short-circuited the system.

A big problem with bulls is keeping them apart and where they should be. They are so big they can jump or walk over most gates, fences, dykes or hedges. Others simply put their head down and bulldoze any obstacles out of the way.

Most bulls stay put because they haven't learnt such habits and don't know their own strength. Once they find out they can go where they please there is no stopping them, other than by keeping them confined to a bullpen or slaughtering them.

The trail of destruction these bulls can leave behind is both impressive and costly. Splintered wooden gates or buckled metal gates, gaps in dykes, or holes in fences. It all adds up.

Most farmers are concerned that if walkers are injured on their farms, they may be sued. So the secret of success will be to devise a scheme that manages visitors in a way that protects them and farmers.

autumn

5

Market mischief

I like to wean or 'spean' lambs by mid-August, as the ewes have virtually stopped producing milk by then. Instead of being the lambs' primary source of nourishment, the ewes compete with them for good grass and clover. 'A sheep's worst enemy is another sheep.'

While with their ewes, lambs spend most of their day keeping an eye on mum and looking for a chance to suckle. Meanwhile their mothers are munching all the best pasture. Speaned and on their own, lambs spend a lot more time grazing, get the pick of the pasture and fatten more quickly.

Speaning is simply a matter of getting someone to run the sheep into a pen that has a funnel feeding a narrow wooden alley-way, or race, the width of the sheep. As they run up it in single file I operate a shedder gate at the end that separates the ewes into one pen and their lambs into another.

That's probably the cruellest thing I ever do to my sheep. For the first couple of nights the air is filled with the noise of lambs bleating for their mothers and ewes bleating for their lambs. But hunger soon wins and by the third day most settle down to their independence and the ewes enjoy a well-earned rest after a summer spent rearing lambs.

Once the lambs are speaned, the next task is to separate the ewe lambs from the wethers and draw them into even-sized batches or 'draws'. You would be amazed at how important that is. Big lambs make small lambs look much smaller when they run side by side. However, a draw of evenly matched, smaller lambs looks larger when there aren't any bigger ones to compare them with. Then I tidy them up by shearing away any soiled wool on their backsides. Wet conditions and lush grass can lead to scouring or diarrhoea that leads to messy rear-ends.

Finally, I dose them for stomach worms and put them onto good pasture, such as silage aftermaths. That's the lush regrowth that comes after the silage crop has been removed and can fatten most lambs within a month to six weeks of speaning.

As they settle down after speaning, I go through the wethers every fortnight and draw off the fat ones that are ready to go to the abattoir. (Wethers are ram lambs that were castrated just after birth in order to prevent indiscriminate breeding.)

Drawing lambs for slaughter is one of the downsides of farming. All farmers rear animals that will ultimately be slaughtered. We all care for our animals to the best of our ability, but at the end of the day farming is a business with little scope for sentiment.

We rear livestock to sell, to bring in enough money to take care of the family, as well as the breeding stock on the farm. On a hill farm such as mine, most of our income arrives in the autumn when we sell our lambs and suckled calves. With the exception of the wool cheque there has usually been no income for five or six months. I can tell you that while the money stops coming in, the bills don't. So while I like my lambs and care for them as best as I can, it's always a relief to sell the first of them to bring in badly needed cash.

Quite a few of the lambs I draw off are well known to me. I may have found them suffering from hypothermia and revived them in my old barrel heater. They may even have spent a few days in a snug bale-pen in my lambing shed with my wife bottle-feeding them extra milk till the weather improved.

Many have distinct characters or unique markings. I can always describe many of the eventful lives of the lambs I draw for slaughter, but part of the secret of a good farmer is not to get too emotionally involved with his stock.

Until recently, I mostly produced Scotch-mule ewe-lambs, the result of crossing a blue-face Leicester tup with Scottish blackface ewes. They are very prolific and make ideal breeding sheep that lowland sheep farmers prefer.

Every year, from about the middle of August till the end of September, sheep farmers from all over Britain attend huge sales of mule ewe-lambs to buy their breeding replacements. Such sales used to last a couple of days and sold up to twenty thousand ewe lambs a day.

To attract the attention of the buyers we dress our sheep. An ideal mule should be big, long, have a bold head with brown patches, large erect ears and a Leicester-type fleece with the wool hanging in tight ringlets or purls as we call them. Dressing is all about enhancing those features.

The belly wool is shorn off to increase the clearance between belly and ground and thus make them look bigger. We remove the wool under the chin and at the front of the neck to make the neck look longer and give the illusion of a longer sheep. Then they are dipped in solutions of colorants and fleece texturisers to make the wool hang perfectly in just the right shade of brown.

The fine hairs inside their ears are carefully trimmed to make their lugs look bigger. It's an old trick that encourages sheep to hold their lugs erect making them look more alert. Then their heads, faces and back legs are shaved. White hairs are longer than brown ones, so shaving makes all the hairs the same length. That gives the sheep darker heads and back legs with more prominent brown patches.

It may all appear a load of nonsense and does nothing to improve the sheep, but it catches the buyers' attention and that can be the difference between a good price and a bad one. Just watch how the lasses use lipstick, mascara, make-up and hairdo to catch the lads' attention at a dance!

Few of us can afford to have concrete in our sheep pens, or buchts as we call them, so it's important not to churn them up in wet weather. Once the ground is churned into mud, it's impossible to keep sheep clean. Every time lambs are being prepared for sale they bunch together and jump on top of one another, smearing muddy hooves on woolly backs. Apart from spoiling their appearance for the sale ring, strict hygiene rules nowadays prevent dirty lambs from being slaughtered. Fortunately the buchts were bone dry that first August and my lambs were dressed in ideal conditions.

Cha and I were discussing the value of the ewe lambs I was about to send to the sale when suddenly the air was filled with the drone of Mac's lorry labouring up my steep farm road. Mac's a fine character and a tremendous diesel mechanic, but a lousy lorry driver.

Corners of buildings are doomed as he catches his container on them. Gates and doors are smashed to splinters as he attempts to reverse. Grass verges are churned to mud by spinning wheels. So Mac's noisy arrival was the signal for the start of ten minutes of anxious shouting as messages of guidance were relayed to him. And much laughing at the usual lurid comments and wisecracks he shouted back.

Mac served in the army, and many of us reckon he was in the tank division the way he drives his lorry. He has eyes like a hawk and is always on the lookout for ropes and canvas straps that have fallen off the back of other lorries. Whenever he spies such bounty, he immediately pulls up to retrieve it, and many a temporary traffic jam on our country roads have been caused by such misadventures.

Eventually we had him in place at the gateway to the buchts and the big loading ramp was lowered. As we set about scattering bags of sawdust on the decks of the lorry to help keep the sheep clean, we were brought up to date on the local gossip.

Most folk would reckon that my farm is isolated. It sits on top of a hill, with panoramic views all round, yet there are only three farmhouses and two shepherd's cottages in sight within a radius of five miles. Even my next-door neighbour, although a mere one-and-a-half miles away as the crow flies, is over two miles by road.

Most of the time the untrained eye never sees a soul from dawn till dusk. But if you look more closely the area is a hive of activity. Groups of sheep bunching together on the hillside give away the movement of a shepherd. You might not be able to see him, but he is out there somewhere checking his flock. Sounds of cattle roaring and the occasional shouting are sure signs of cattle being fed.

As farmers use their eyes more than townsfolk, they notice vehicles moving about farm and country roads. Just as the sight of the vet's car tells us a neighbour has a sick animal, the little red knackery lorry proclaims the beast didn't survive. Blacksmiths' pick-ups or machinery dealers' vans alert us to a breakdown somewhere.

Certain cars are a sign a sales rep is calling and the factor's Land Rover Discovery might hint that a rent negotiation is under way, or some improvement planned.

If a livestock lorry has been seen and your neighbour hasn't mentioned it, you can be sure he got a bad price at the market. And if the lorry returns that afternoon, you know prices were so bad he decided not to sell, and brought the stock home again.

Farming communities are very tight-knit and often interrelated. It used to be almost impossible for something to happen without someone finding out and passing on the details. Although gossip that distorts simple events into ripping yarns isn't pleasant for those concerned, it has to be accepted as part of country life.

I have learned that the secret of living in the country is to watch what you say to folk. Nine times out of ten, if you speak ill of someone, it's probably their cousin or in-law you have confided in. Mind you, if someone isn't keeping well, the jungle drums soon start beating and friends and neighbours come rallying round. It's always nice to have people offering a helping hand. Indeed, gossip and loss of privacy are a small price to pay to be part of a genuinely caring community.

Contrast that with city life where people often don't even know their neighbour's name, never mind speaking to them. Old folk can die alone without anyone noticing. There's a lot to be said for a good blether spiced with a bit of concerned enquiry as well as gossip.

Sadly, modern farming is becoming a very lonely way of life. At one time, there were lots of workers housed in a farm's cottages. They coped with the round of seasonal tasks like hoeing turnips, haymaking or harvest.

Smaller farms that couldn't afford to hire hands 'neighboured' each other at tasks like sheep clipping. By that I mean they took it in turn to help each other. Many hands make light work and many a tedious chore became more of a social gathering. Large suppers in the farmhouse kitchen often gave way to an impromptu ceilidh. Such events are now almost a thing of the past.

Large hill farms are too short of staff and busy to help their neighbours, while smaller units find it simpler to plod away themselves or hire a gang of contract shearers. There are now fewer opportunities for social contact with other farmers.

Years ago, before the advent of artificial insemination, small farmers hired bulls, stallions or boars. That involved walking a cow, sow or mare in season to a nearby farm to be served for a fee. There was always time to blether before walking your charge home and meeting others on the way.

It was a common practice to lend equipment either to those who couldn't afford it or others who needed more machines to speed up the work. The golden rule in those days was that you should always return equipment in better condition than you received it. That often involved a short trip to the blacksmith for a repair and a good blether before taking it back.

There's little chance to glean any tittle-tattle these days. We have either got a complete range of equipment or we hire a contractor to do the job. Modern contractors must work their machinery hard to make a profit so, as with everyone else involved in farming, they don't have time to chat.

Telephones, faxes and modern selling systems have made hundreds of gossiping sales reps redundant. Modern postmen are always in a rush racing their red vans up lanes in a cloud of dust.

So, more and more, farmers are becoming isolated and that isn't helped by the fact that many wives are forced to take jobs away from the farm. It all makes for a long, lonely and often dreich day.

Farmers are sociable like everybody else and enjoy company. Somebody to share a joke, moan or boast with can make all the difference. Friendly faces are rapidly becoming very scarce around modern farmsteads.

Mac is in the privileged position of calling at many different farms in the district and seeing just what's going on. Also, because he's at the markets every day, he knows exactly what prices everyone's been getting.

'What's the difference between roast beef and pea soup?' he asked us. After a moment of silence he replied, 'anyone can roast beef.' That was his other great strength, he was a fund of jokes. After we had loaded the sheep, Cha climbed into the lorry cab with Mac so that he could help unload and pen the sheep at the market. I went to get washed and changed before following them in my car.

The market as usual was bursting at the seams. It's a colourful place, populated by a myriad of characters. There are some well-dressed affluent farmers as well as many well-dressed ones trying to appear affluent, who spend much of their time avoiding sales reps so they don't have to pay last month's accounts.

Mingling among them are some of the smelliest, worst-dressed farmers who are probably the most affluent of all. And in the background there is the constant natter of the auctioneer as he cajoles bids out of reluctant buyers.

It's the duty of the shepherd or owner to stay with his sheep till they are sold. So while the auction ring is packed with buyers and spectators, the pens outside are just as busy with those tending their sheep.

That's where the real crack is. Apart from the usual gossip, those who are outside spend a lot of time looking at the different pens of sheep. Often there are arguments about which is the best pen. Some sheep have that special glint in their eyes. Others may have good skins or dark heads. Some are well prepared while others are just plain vermin.

Selling sheep is a matter of honour, where reputations are made or broken. He who tops a sale has just cause to puff up his chest and walk proud all day.

Farmers are price takers rather than price makers. Most folk fix their prices but farmers tend to sell by auction. In other words, farmers go to market and ask 'what will you give me for my produce?' Auctions are the best way of establishing the true value of a commodity. Snag is, a large part of our income is determined by a few minutes in the auction ring. You only sell once, so it has to be done right.

Stock is presented for sale in their best bloom. Well fed and carefully groomed they should look their very best on sale day. Idea is to make them look sharp and healthy as they move round the ring. Some farmers stand at the gate into the ring and tap the floor with their stick as the sheep enter. That makes the sheep skip and bounce to avoid that tapping stick, making them look fit and strong.

Another trick is to keep the best animals to the outside of the bunch as they walk round. Easier said than done! It's amazing how the ugliest always manage to parade proudly in full view of prospective buyers. But it's the patter and play-acting that's often the main part of the sale.

A whole host of subtle statements are made to catch the gullible and unwary. 'Never been below a thousand feet', suggests that the sheep will soon double in size if they're moved to lowland pastures. It's amazing how many farmers claim to have no land below a thousand feet!

'Altering kinds' or 'they'll go on and do' are phrases used to encourage bids for inferior animals. Bids vary from an open shout or wave of the hand to a secretive wink, flick of the head or twitch of a finger. Sometimes merely looking at the auctioneer is taken as a bid.

Often there's only one bidder and the auctioneer may 'run him up' to get a fair price. Auctioneers, of course, only need one foolish bidder to make a brisk trade. 'I have it twice bid, but I'll take yours sir', is a favourite to reassure a mug that there's some-one else bidding. As an auctioneer once remarked to me, 'to get a good price takes two bidders . . . you and me!' Not that the buyers are innocent either. They're quick to announce faults they have spotted.

A good or bad trade can make a big difference to the bank account, and it's an education to watch some farmers trying to squeeze the last pound out of the buyers. A good auctioneer always wants to do his best for his customer as the bigger the price the more commission he earns. But some farmers do their own cabaret act to help the auctioneer. 'Naw. Can't be done at that price. Unthinkable! That's giving them away.'

He knows, the auctioneer knows and the crowd knows that he's kidding, but somehow it works. Another bid is made and sometimes it can set the whole ringside off again. I have often seen farmers add several pounds a head to a pen of lambs by doing his hand up, head-shaking act.

Mind you, I have never heard of anything to top an act I once heard about. Helping the farmer bring his lambs into the auction ring were four young lads, going down in size like a set of steps. As the auctioneer started looking for bids the farmer lined his sons up. 'Growing lads', he said. 'They take a lot of feeding so I'm relying on a good trade here today.'

When the bidding slowed down he added, 'and there are another two at home with their mother.' That was worth another couple of pounds. Again the auctioneer raised the hammer when the farmer raised his hand, 'And there's another one on the way.' That brought the house down and raised another bid.

Auction marts were the lifeblood of farmers and most large towns in Scotland had one. They used to be located in town, but caused traffic jams on market day as livestock lorries queued with their animals. Times change and most auctioning companies sold their town premises to supermarkets or developers and replaced them with modern marts conveniently sited next to motorways and bypasses. Despite such big investments, livestock markets are going through difficult times. Many have closed or merged and even more could disappear.

Markets were the focus of farm business as well as playing an important social role. All manner of farm produce was bought and sold through auctioneers, monthly accounts with feed firms and such like were settled and new deals struck. Sales reps mingled with the farmers touting for new business, while farmers' wives did their weekly shopping in town.

Lunches in the market restaurant were always wholesome and good value for money. Auction marts were the gossip machinery of the countryside, where many a trivial tale grew to be a major scandal. Sadly that's all under threat in our fast-changing world. Foot-and-mouth taught us the importance of biosecurity. Mixing animals from different farms in market pens is a sure way of spreading diseases.

Foot-and-mouth culls and lack of profitability have seen a decline in the number of sheep and cattle produced on farms. Fewer animals lead to less commission for auctioneers. As with farming, mart costs keep rising and these have to be passed on in higher commission charges.

Many farmers have stopped using the markets and now supply their livestock directly to abattoirs. Others prefer private deals where animals move directly from one farm to another and avoid the problems of stress and spreading disease.

Above all else, few of us now have the time to go to market as it can involve a long day. Animals are often loaded onto the lorry first thing in the morning. After breakfast and a change of clothes you have to drive to market. Often the animals do not enter the auction ring until mid-afternoon, so you don't get back home till teatime. Matters are made worse on the bad days wasted when prices are low and you decide not to sell but bring the animals back home. There will always be a need for markets but sadly there will only be a handful of big ones left in the future.

When sheep or cattle are sold we have a custom called the luck penny. Traditionally the seller gave the buyer a penny. The buyer would then spit on it and put it in his pocket. That little ritual makes the stock lucky. Times change and nowadays it's fivers and tenners rather than pennies that change hands. I drew cash from the auctioneers' office and gave my various buyers their luck penny before heading off in search of Cha to give him a lift home. As usual he was ensconced in the market bar, holding forth with all the gossip and jokes he had only recently gleaned from Mac.

My sale of lambs had gone well and to celebrate my good fortune I arranged to meet Cha and Big Tam later that evening for a pint in our local. It's a small hotel that caters for salmon fishermen and it was full of English fishers that night.

We waited to be served as they hogged the bar chattering about flies, lures and ones that got away. Soon Cha was the centre of attention as he knowingly advised the visitors where the best pools and lies were. Desperate for local knowledge, they gratefully plied us with drinks.

In the taxi home I told Cha that I had never realised he was an expert fisherman. He just winked and replied, 'You only need a little local knowledge of the river to catch a bunch of fishermen.'

6

Harvest hostilities

After peewits, swallows are my favourite birds. One can't help but admire them for undertaking those long migrations, all the way from Africa, just to suffer another of our dreich, wet summers.

Whatever, I look forward to their arrival as it usually heralds the start of summer. After a summer of the swallows' chattering company I'm always sad to see them go in the autumn. They're real little busybodies. In the morning they sit on the telephone wire twittering away, discussing their plans for the day and catching up on any gossip. Once they're sure I'm awake, they swoop and soar around the farm buildings till dusk, gathering flies for their hungry broods.

Snag with swallows is the mess they make, particularly in the garage. For years we had a swallow's nest in one of the rafters. While the chicks and the mother bird weren't really a problem, the male swallow roosted at night on the strip light above the car. Every morning there were swallow droppings on the bonnet. What a mess they made considering they are only little birds! You would think that hens had roosted on my car.

Invariably, I had to hose the mess off before going anywhere. Since nine journeys out of ten I'm in a rush, my shoes and trousers often got soaked. Easiest solution would have been to knock the nest down when they started to build it, but it seemed a shame to put all their hard labour of gathering mud to waste.

Then I employed a successful new tactic to discourage our

summer visitors from using the garage as a 'des res'. I bought a large plastic owl with big, fierce, staring eyes and put him on that strip light. The idea came from a dairy farmer friend who was pestered with sparrows in his cowshed leaving droppings in feed troughs. Once he installed his owl the sparrows disappeared.

The secret of success is to keep the eyes well polished and bright, as it's the staring eyes that scare small birds away. The beauty of keeping a plastic owl in my garage is that it doesn't need feeding, doesn't stray and doesn't leave droppings on the car.

If only pigeons and rooks were as easy to scare off when they attack ripening fields of grain. August signals the beginning of the annual war with those pests, which appear in their hundreds.

The outgoing tenant had sown seven acres of oats that I took over at valuation. For many years I used to have about forty acres of barley that kept me self-sufficient in grain and straw. I crushed the grain and fed it to my livestock during the winter, while the straw was either fed to my cattle or used as bedding. That all stopped in the early nineties in response to poor grain and straw prices. I worked out it was cheaper to buy it rather than attempt to grow it on my high-lying farm.

The amount of grain pigeons or doos can consume when unchecked is enormous and could even lead to a harvest failure. The rules of this annual war are that there are no rules and anything goes.

The system is loosely based on the futile concept of chasing them onto a field belonging to a neighbour, who immediately chases them back. It seemed to me that my fields were held in increasingly high esteem by pigeons and crows with a discerning palate and that the entire bird population preferred my crops to my neighbour's.

Was it something to do with the soil, or the climate, that brought out some special gourmet flavour in my barley? Or was it the presence of a variety of uncontrolled weeds that offered a divergence of flavours like a side salad to the main course? I never knew, but of one thing I was certain, I definitely got more than my fair share of *columba palumbus*, or should I say, cushat doos!

It's not the grain they ate that upset me, but rather the amount they wasted with their feet trampling the heads of grain into the ground. Even more harassing was their attitude to mere farmers trying to persuade them to eat elsewhere.

Automatic bird scarers, bangers, kites that resemble hawks, scarecrows and flapping polythene fertiliser bags on stakes all seemed to grow less effective every year.

Readers should be aware of the futility of making scarecrows. Hours can be spent trying to make a menacing-looking human intent on killing pigeons, yet those wily creatures regarded such creations with contempt, realising that as it was static it couldn't harm them. Indeed, on several occasions I have seen birds perched on top of scarecrows.

Even more disappointing was their response to bangers. Initially they reacted by flying round the field a few times before settling, but after a few harmless bangs they remained unperturbed except for the occasional highly-strung novice that might fly ten yards away from the irritating sound.

The only thing those airborne vacuum-cleaners were genuinely frightened of was a man with a shotgun over his arm. Problem was, even if you had the time, how to get near enough to fire a shot? You would have thought that with their carefree kamikaze attitude to life, that shooting them would be easy. Not so!

They always had sentries posted to warn of my stealthy approach and, after casually observing where I had 'hidden' myself, proceeded to feed in the farthest-away corner of another field.

Even sophisticated attempts to foil them failed miserably. One ruse that always baffled me was the way they could count, for instance, if three people walked up to a proposed hide, but only two left, they still knew that someone was left behind.

Once I had successfully hidden myself the real test began, a test of patience and nerves. They tested my patience and I tested their nerves. Now patience was never one of my strong points. Eventually through the boredom of waiting and nothing happening, I would fall asleep, only to awaken to the sound of the cawing and cooing of my bloated feathered enemies preening themselves after a good feed. The final test of man's supremacy over birds failed miserably as I missed with both barrels.

Then by some strange but effective means of communication, every bird in the district knew that I had given up and gone home, and confidently returned to resume the annual feast.

Vast new areas of inaccessible, but ideal, pigeon-nesting sites were created with increased conifer plantations. Rooks also increased in number because nobody controls the rookeries by shooting as they used to. And a series of mild winters helped pigeons and crows reach levels at which they are now a real nuisance.

That first harvest was an easy one due to near-drought conditions. Normally a Scottish harvest yields a fair proportion of moist grain that could go mouldy if not properly dried. Drying grain, so that it is fit for storage, is expensive thanks to the high cost of fuel. Fortunately, that year the crops came into the stores in perfect condition and most farm dryers stood idle.

My small harvest was destined for animal feed so instead of sending the grain away to be dried I used to mix in small amounts of propionic acid that stopped it going mouldy and preserved it.

I had managed to buy a well-maintained, old combine at a machinery sale in Lanark for £460. Compared to modern machines it was small. Today's high-tech giants can cut upwards of twenty-two feet at a time and cost well in excess of £100,000. My ancient relic could only manage eight feet six inches at a time but that was adequate for my acreage. Two years later I bought an identical, but older model for £100. With spares virtually unobtainable that hundred quid proved to be a good investment. Every time I had a breakdown I stripped parts off the old one.

As I said, I used to grow about forty acres of barley, so with contractors charging £20 an acre for combining, my investment paid for itself in a couple of years.

Another advantage of having a combine is that you don't have to wait on the contractor. There's nothing more frustrating than watching a good week go by knowing the contractor is working elsewhere and won't arrive till the weather breaks.

Mind you, it wasn't all plain sailing.

Combine breakdowns are made more frustrating by the location of the broken part. It always seemed inaccessible and invariably in some dark, dusty or greasy recess that left you caked with a mixture of grease and itchy dust.

Another drawback was the lack of a cab. Modern combines have air-conditioned cabs, complete with radios and every conceivable electronic gauge or gadget. My trusty machine had none of that. I sat there in the full heat of the day, in a haze of itchy dust, longing for a shower and an ice-cold beer in the shade.

Next to me, at ear level, was the engine and as the radiator was at the far end, the fan constantly blew burnt oil and diesel fumes over me. At the end of a long, dusty, smelly day with the noise of that engine still humming in my ear I was well and truly puggled.

Then there were the wet harvests that could turn into a nightmare. Heavy rain flattens the crops and once the heads of grain are on the ground they seldom dry properly and soon start to sprout.

Even standing grain isn't safe. Over-ripe heads of barley are shaken by the wind and eventually fall to the ground. As a wet autumn progresses, weeds, particularly grass, keep growing and envelop the drooping heads of grain in a damp environment. It then takes extra hours of sun and wind to dry the dew that stubbornly clings to that green mat.

Damp crops cause many problems. Combines that can work non-stop without a hitch in sunny weather become unreliable. Lumps of damp straw block the intake to the threshing mechanism. Damp grain clogs up the augers and elevators that move it around the combine to the holding tank.

Cutting close to the ground when harvesting crops that have been flattened inevitably leads to stones being picked up as well. Breakages and blockages soon have most of us bad-tempered and frustrated.

As the sky darkens, threatening yet another shower, it's always tempting to drive the combine faster than the difficult conditions will allow. End result is usually another breakdown and a miserable farmer driving his combine home in pouring rain.

On top of the hassle there's also the cost to consider. Lower yields through lost grain. Increased fuel costs to dry the damp grain and poorer prices for lower quality.

Farming fortunes depend on the weather more than politicians and subsidies. After the extra fuel costs and repair bills are set against the lower yields and poorer prices in a wet harvest there is often a loss.

That first harvest was bliss and I easily combined those seven acres in a day. The only time things became a bit fraught was when Cha manoeuvred the tractor and trailer alongside to collect the grain that had accumulated in the combine's bulk tank.

Cha makes a point of looking anywhere but at the combine. If I slowed down to allow the combine to cope with a particularly thick patch, he wouldn't notice but drive on. That left me frantically trying to stop all the golden grain pouring to the ground.

Similarly, his attempts at changing gear would have the tractor stationary and the combine overtaking and pouring grain over his tractor cab instead of into the trailer. Big Tam assured me later that Cha's attempts at reversing the trailer to the barn door were just as nerve-racking.

I once had a mishap with my Land Rover when it slid down a wet, slippery bank and lodged against a thorn tree. Cha was summoned to tow me out of my predicament with a tractor. As usual he was lighting a cigarette, instead of looking behind, as he towed me towards a gateway. As a result, he was blissfully unaware that the Land Rover wasn't following his tractor in a straight line, but sliding sideways down that slippery bank. Despite frantically blowing my horn to warn him of my dilemma, he drove through the gateway and towed the Land Rover straight into the gatepost.

Another similar incident occurred one winter, when his wife was unable to drive her car up his steep, snow-covered road. She summoned him to tow her up the road with his tractor, which he proceeded to do without looking behind him.

Unfortunately, his wife hadn't switched on the engine and, as a result, the steering was locked. She found herself in a similar predicament to the one I had been in, except her car was veering up onto a steep bank on the topside of the farm road.

Fortunately, on this occasion, he looked back in time to see his wife's car had climbed high up the bank and was in danger of toppling over. As Tam loved to recall, that left her 'nursing her wrath to keep it warm'.

Whenever Tam reminds him of that folly, Cha always recites an unfortunate tale that befell Tam. His car ran out of diesel one afternoon as he was leaving my farm. As he was in a rush to get home to attend a Burns supper that evening, we put a couple of gallons of red diesel in his tank and then bled his engine to get him going again.

With hindsight, we should have taken the time to go to the local garage to fetch regular diesel, that has had the duty paid, rather than use the red stuff that is sold to farmers duty free.

Being a law-abiding citizen, Tam became alarmed when Cha reminded him that Customs officers regularly carried out spot checks on diesel cars and tested them for red diesel being used illegally. His alarm was always increased by Cha's reminder that traces of red diesel persisted for months in the tank, and that the tests would always detect it. 'Aye, they'll stop you, test your diesel and find you out. Then the customs officer will put his hand on your car's bonnet and declare that he is seizing your vehicle in the name of Her Majesty', he would solemnly advise. 'Sic a parcel of rogues in a nation', he would quote from Burns, to drive his point home.

Once all the grain was safely in the store we then had to bale the straw, which is used for cattle feed during the winter.

Many is the time I have had to attend the parish kirk's harvest-thanksgiving service with half my grain crop lying uncut because of wet weather, but that year we beat the minister to it.

A harvest safely in store is the cue for rats to come into the farm buildings for the winter. Most of them happily spend the summer in fields and hedgerows until food starts to dwindle and colder weather arrives. But as the nights draw in they make their way along dykes, riverbanks and burns in search of a cosy barn. Once they are installed there for the winter they are hard to control.

Anyone with experience of the pests will know the term 'dirty rat' is a true description. Not content to burrow through a stack of straw bales in search of grain or likely nest sites, they also love to nibble needlessly through the strings that bind the bales together. Polypropylene string is tasteless, of no nutritive value and rarely used for nest building, yet rats will gnaw through every string in a stack of bales. There's nothing worse than lifting a big, 250-kilo bale with the tractor loader and watch it fall to bits for want of string. The result is a never-ending mass of loose, dusty straw that has to be pitchforked onto trailers, then pitchforked off again instead of being conveniently handled by the hydraulic loader. Driving that sort of load across a windy yard leaves a trail of loose straw blowing in the wind.

Rats also attack electric cables resulting in fuses blowing and the risk of fire. How many farm fires, I wonder, have been started by electrical faults as a result of rat-damaged cables? They'll also tackle timber, mortar and even concrete.

Jute sackcloth or paper bags are other tasteless products rats love to gnaw, and they have an infuriating habit of gnawing holes in the corner of feed bags. So when the bag is slung over your shoulder and carried across the yard, it leaves a trail of foodstuff that has to be swept up and then dumped because it is contaminated with dirt and small stones.

Despite being a strapping farmer, I am a big feartie when it comes to rats. As a lad I well remember how they squeaked and scuttled everywhere when you went into the barn at night. It fairly made my hairs stand up on the back of my neck. They dived into well-polished boltholes in the thick mortar walls or under the flagstones that paved the floor. Others scrambled frantically along the rafters or door lintel and occasionally fell on to my head and shoulders. Many are the times I have nearly grabbed one in the poor light of dawn as I went to lift a bale.

After a couple of near misses of that nature I soon learned to whistle loudly as I crossed the yard, as well as give the barn door a good long rattle before entering. Thus warned, the rats had time to make themselves scarce and get out of sight. Only when all the scampering of little feet on loft floorboards had subsided did I enter.

My worst fright ever was when I was loading straw bales on to a trailer and a startled rat ran up the leg of my boiler suit. Fortunately it scuttled back down just as quickly, but left me breathless and shaken for the rest of the morning. Then there was the time I was rolling back the large plastic sheet that covers the silage pit when I startled a rat that ran over my boots to escape. I got such a fright I fell ten feet off the pit and hurt my shoulder.

Traditional farm buildings, with their thick stone and mortar walls, were ideal havens for rats. Over the years, those buildings have gradually been demolished and replaced with modern sheds with concrete floors and walls. So there are now few hiding places for rats.

The biggest danger from rats is their droppings and urine that contaminate animal feed and transmit disease. Their urine on bales or sacks transmits the killer Weils disease (leptospirosis) to humans. For that reason alone I always wear rubber gloves when working in such conditions.

Over the years I have fought hard to get rid of rats. Holes were blocked with a mixture of broken glass and cement or tin plate. All kinds of poisons and traps have been used. Adequate poisoned bait should be left at strategic points round the buildings. Best method is to leave it in drainage pipes to keep it dry.

Some poisoned bait comes in little plastic bags. That way it stays fresh till the inquisitive rats open the bags themselves.

The big problem with farm buildings is that there's food everywhere. Grain in the lofts or bins, animal feed in the barn and sheds and small amounts of unthreshed grain in among the stacks of straw. In such instances, poisoned bait and traps are a waste of time. Why should a rat risk its life when there's a huge pile of delicious grain to be guzzled?

My secret weapon is Racumin tracking powder. I place a two-inch-wide layer inside or across the entrance to rat holes, or as one-foot patches in a rat run. Another good spot for laying the stuff is at the holes gnawed through timbers in the eaves of a roof. Rats need water daily and roof guttering is a favourite spot for a secret drink. The tracking powder sticks to their fur and a fatal dose is licked off and swallowed when they groom themselves.

So, despite the mess those dirty rats make, their downfall is that they keep themselves spotlessly clean.

Mind you, with modern buildings and poisons, rats aren't the problem they once were. Plagues of them used to infest the stacks of oat sheaves. When the travelling threshing mill came, a small net was erected round the stack to keep the rats from escaping and a few terriers were put in.

As the day's threshing wore on the enclosed area became a cacophony of barking and squealing, mingled with the shouts of laddies with sticks. Woe-betide those who didn't bother to tie the bottom of their trouser legs to keep the rats out.

Sometimes, when all else has failed, I resort to an old-fashioned cage trap that I bait with a chocolate biscuit. Like me, rats can't resist such a treat and I often find it securely caught the next morning.

I had the good fortune one winter to have a large stoat spend a few months around the farm buildings. That fairly did the trick as it fed on rats and scared the rest away. I am not so sure that farm cats are all that effective and often think they only make rats lie low and keep out of sight.

Farm cats are a rough, tough lot and not a bit like domesticated pussycats. Many of them are half-wild and most live off what they catch. Young rabbits, small birds, mice and occasionally a rat make up their daily menu. Most of the cat's time is spent hunting in hedgerows and woods. Not for them the luxury of a tin of cat food in the kitchen.

That's not to say we don't leave food out for them, but it's only a small amount of dog meal that's been steeped in boiling water. Snag with farm cats is that if they are too well fed they soon breed in large numbers. If the food supply is limited, surplus cats drift off to other farms when the hunting becomes poor.

Too many cats can be bad. There are the problems with sleepless nights as you lie in bed listening to their wailing courtship and ensuing fights. Then there is the daily horror of removing cat droppings from a blocked bruiser, the machine that crushes grain, due to the cat's distorted perception of hygiene whereby it diligently buries its excrement in heaps of barley. That also spreads toxoplasmosis. It's a disease carried by young cats that causes abortion in sheep.

The shriek of a cat as you accidentally stand on its foot or tail, or shut the barn door on it, is nerve shattering. The trail of muddy paw prints over a car bonnet after a cat has had a nap above the warm engine is also annoying.

The real test of wills comes when they learn that a simpler method of feeding is to patiently wait at the back door and dash into the kitchen to grab whatever is going rather than the dubious exercise of tackling an aggressive rat.

That's when all hell can break loose resulting in torn curtains and smashed crockery. Occasionally they have roast chicken, leg of lamb or a piece of beef, so it's worth waiting for. Trouble is that you don't always see them, but from under bushes and round corners, feline eyes are constantly watching that back door.

Despite all that, we did have a house cat, called Fluff, that was found abandoned as a kitten by my youngest daughter and brought into the house. It was touch and go whether Fluff would live. The half-starved wee mite spent the first week sleeping in a cardboard box next to the Rayburn cooker, but warm milk and titbits of meat soon revived her. It goes without saying that, once recovered, there was no way our daughter would allow us to evict Fluff.

Realising the privileged position she enjoyed, Fluff became a model house-trained cat and part of the family. She went on to produce a fine set of six kittens that prompted a visit to the vet to have her neutered. Fluff's half-grown kittens were put in the barn to learn to run outside with the rest of the farm cats.

I remember once driving to town on an errand when the car started making an unusual noise. So I lifted the bonnet to investigate the problem and found one of Fluff's kittens. Attracted by the warmth of the engine it had somehow crawled on top of it. Caught napping it had enjoyed a wee hurl into town and it was the kitten, not the engine, that had made the unusual noise.

7

The mating game

There are about fifty main breeds of sheep in the United Kingdom and a similar number of rare breeds, imported breeds, hybrids and half-breeds.

Breeds were developed over generations to suit a particular environment. Blackfaces, or blackies as we call them, those hill ewes with horns, have been bred for the wet, west of Scotland. Then there are Swaledales that suit the fells of the Lake District, or South Country Cheviots from the drier hills on the south-east of Scotland. There are also big, meaty down breeds like the Suffolk or Hampshire and on it goes.

My farming system is a lot less complicated since the happy day I sold off my blackie ewes and replaced them with mules. An Environmentally Sensitive Area (ESA) heather-regeneration programme started in the late nineties prompted the sale of my blackies and the government pays me £35 a year for each one removed. After several years of this inspired scheme I can confide that non-existent blackies are easier to work with than real ones.

Blackies didn't adapt well to my farm's spartan conditions. Matters always came to a head at lambing time when they would get stuck giving birth to a big single lamb or abandon a weak pair of twins to suckle rushes on an exposed knowe. Such tragedies often ended in something closely resembling a fox-hunt as my dogs gave chase followed by the ritual of lifting a sodden ewe out of the burn and carrying her back up a steep glen.

Once another lamb was fostered on there followed the quaint tradition of getting her and her lamb from the lambing shed to the adjacent field. Whilst her lamb suckled the tractor drawbar she would stamp her hooves at the dogs, skip into the yard, jump over the garden dyke and once again lead a wild chase back to the burn.

Happily those days are now behind me. Better still is the fact that I no longer have to buy and work with blue-face Leicester tups. The only positive thing that I can say about the breed is that their fine, lustrous wool is extremely valuable. It's also very scarce as few Leicesters in my experience live long enough to be shorn! I have spent many a weary hour digging in hard ground to lay the brutes to rest as they are in a class of their own when it comes to dying!

Most sheep are fickle creatures and die from a hundred-and-one different diseases, but the Leicester constantly finds new ways to shuffle off this mortal coil. It is a low-ground breed that is often excessively fed prior to sale and as a result adapts badly to working on wet and windy hill farms. One of the reasons it is often so expensive is that there simply aren't enough replacements to go round.

Sheep lose about 80 per cent of their body heat through their ears. Hardy sheep like the South Country Cheviot, Herdwicks or dare I mention them, blackies, have small ears whilst the blue-faced Leicester has about the biggest. Big, erect lugs and a fine fleece make them one of the coldest breeds known to man. Their brief lives are eked out sheltering behind dykes with arched backs.

By a strange quirk of nature the blackie and blueface click when mated and produce the mule. I suppose it's a case of two extreme types producing maximum hybrid vigour rather like when South African farmers cross Brahman bulls with Hereford cows.

Mule ewes are undoubtedly idiot proof and reliable. Without too much effort on my part they produce large crops of well-grown lambs. When my intervention is required at lambing they are docile and easily handled. I can think of no better cross for commercial sheep farmers.

Mind you, mule breeders are unusual people. I suppose you need to be unusual to want to work with blackies and bluefaces. Those strange people happily spend their days needlessly clipping bellies, opening out necks, shaving heads and legs, snipping out unwanted hair inside lugs, repeatedly dipping to colour and purl fleeces and finally washing faces. Such strange practices add nothing to the mule's performance but are done in the name of presentation and marketing.

I am glad that I am no longer part of all that nonsense. Nowadays I prefer to buy my mules rather than breed them, safe in the knowledge that no matter how much the breeders dress them up they can't conceal the fact that it is an outstanding cross.

In the autumn the surplus breeding stock in the form of five-year-old ewes that are getting too old to survive another year on the high hills, as well as those ewe lambs not good enough to breed pure, are sold to lower-lying upland-farms to be crossed. Those crossbred ewe lambs are then sold on to low-ground farms to be crossed with meaty, terminal sires like the Suffolk.

Such a system utilises all the land resources to best advantage as well as making the maximum use of hybrid vigour with all the benefits of faster growth rates and improved fertility.

Hill-farming is governed by the amount of animals that can be wintered. There is always plenty of grass in the middle of summer, but reserves have to be left on the hill to allow the breeding stock to survive the winter. It's the same for the cattle. The size of the herd is determined by the amount of fodder that can be made to keep the beasts fed during winter.

My cattle seldom get out of their sheds until after the middle of May and I always make more than enough silage to feed them until the end of May. That's one of the snags of a hill farm; everything is that little bit later in growing.

Generally there's a temperature drop of about a degree Celsius for every three hundred feet above sea level. My farm lies at about seven hundred and fifty feet so is roughly two-and-a-half degrees colder than a coastal farm just thirty miles away. That same effect often catches hillwalkers unawares. It may be settled where they park the car but, once they've climbed above fifteen-hundred feet, they soon notice the temperature drop.

As with most businesses, the location of a farm makes a big difference to profitability. Some are fortunate to be in the south-west and benefit from the Gulf Stream. Campbeltown and Wigtownshire dairy farmers will have grass growing a month to six weeks earlier than most.

Even having a farm that lies on a slope facing the sun can make all the difference and the advantages gained from such slight variations can be enormous. Some low-lying farms in a favourable district that face the sun can have a short four-to-five month winter. My cattle are often in their sheds by mid-October and sometimes stay there till the end of May. In other words, I can end up feeding my cattle half as long again as better-placed lowland farms.

Most hill farms sell off surplus animals in the autumn so that only the breeding stock is left for the winter. September is a month when hill farms fall silent. Peewits and curlews no longer noisily wheel in the sky chasing crows, sheepdogs or foxes from their young. Almost unnoticed they slip away to their winter quarters. Larks stop chanting on the wing and ewes no longer call for their lambs. It's a time of year when summer visitors leave the high hills before the winter sets in. Hardy hill-grouse remain and call out to the unwary, 'go back, go back, go back!'

Most of the lambs have been gathered in and sold at the sales. Stock-ewe lambs, the best ones kept for breeding replacements, will soon be sent away to lowland farms for the winter. They need good grass to let them grow to their full potential. A hill in winter can be a hungry place and their presence would mean less for the ewes. So at the end of September and in early October you will often see wagons laden with ewe lambs heading for lowland farms. There they stay until early April before being brought home to their hills.

September is also the month when the draft ewes are drawn off for sale. They are mostly five-year-olds and despite having had four lambings they can go on and breed for another couple of years in a kinder environment. Most draft ewes are bought to produce crossbred lambs although some are bought for pure breeding and can be worth a lot more. Good ewes off a top flock are often bought to improve the stock at home and it's a good way of introducing better bloodlines.

I seldom sell such ewes and prefer to keep the older ones separately and feed them a little bit extra during the winter.

Despite that policy I still have cast ewes to sell. They are the ones that are no longer suitable for breeding, often because they are too old, but invariably they have faulty udders or mouths. Ewes that have something wrong with their udders, such as mastitis, are useless. In cold wet weather at lambing time, their lambs can perish very quickly if they don't produce enough milk. So rather than run that risk we cull them.

We also cull sheep with teeth missing because they find it hard to graze properly. Lack of teeth is probably the main reason for culling ewes. Too many sheep start to lose teeth at only five years old while most are broken-mouthed by seven.

Some farmers with better land breed from broken-mouthed ewes, but on our harsh hill farm it would be a catastrophe resulting in starvation and death during the winter. That's why you will often see farmers looking carefully into the mouths of breeding sheep, particularly rams, before they buy them.

It's a real scunner having to part with good sheep because of broken mouths. As Cha used to say, 'thank goodness nobody bothers to look in *my* mouth.'

Breeding ewes need rams, or tups as we call them, and September is the month for tup sales, when the words that never leave many sheep breeders' lips are whisky, beer and tups. Each breed has its own special sales but the big Scottish event is Kelso, held on a Friday in the middle of September. There's been an annual auction of tups in the riverside fields at Springwood Park, beneath Floors Castle, since 1838 and it's now Europe's largest. I have seen days when over six thousand tups have changed hands for £3 million but today's sales probably handle about five thousand. It takes a dozen different auction companies about nine hours to sell them through fifteen auction rings selling simultaneously.

Two rows of large marquees house the pampered princes of the sheep world and each marquee can shade four hundred from the bright autumn sun or shelter them from torrential rain. Kelso can be a cold, wet, miserable outing where the show field turns into a sea of glaur. At the end of each marquee is an auction ring through which the tups are sold. Superstition dictates there is no thirteenth ring so fifteen rings will be numbered one to sixteen.

Most of the main breeds are there. Largest consignment is the Suffolks, with their black face and legs and smoothly contoured fleece. There are usually more than three thousand and they can use ten rings. Although the breed originated in England, breeders from the north-east of Scotland often get the top prices.

A breeder from Lanarkshire may sell his consignment using an auctioneer from Lanark market, to be followed by a Devonshire breeder who will have travelled north with his auctioneer.

You have to get to the sale early in the morning and work out the lie of the land. You then have to work out when and where the sheep of your choice are to be sold. There might be one to come under the hammer in ring ten at eleven o'clock followed by another in ring three at twelve o'clock. Often a couple you are interested in will be sold at the same time in separate rings.

As the day wears on you can become more and more frustrated. With every passing hour yet another friend will cheerfully greet you with news that they are giving them away in such and such a ring. Unfortunately, such information spreads like wildfire so, by the time you have nipped over, so has everyone else. On your return, your neighbour will gleefully announce he's just bought a couple on the cheap when everyone left!

The real hassle begins once you have made your purchases. After waiting in different queues to pay several auctioneers you then had to weave the Land Rover and trailer through the confusion to the appropriate marquees. You can imagine the bedlam as hundreds of vehicles and trailers descend to load up their purchases. That is now a thing of the past as there is a service, involving quad bikes and trailers, that collects the tups and delivers them to your vehicle for a small fee.

After loading up their tups, many drivers then have to gather up their passengers. They're sometimes found admiring a pen of sheep or cracking with a crony, but far more likely in the beer-tent throng. As the afternoon wears on, the tups become bigger and better, or smaller and uglier depending on the tale and how much drink has been consumed.

It was at the bar at Kelso tup sales that I first watched Cha perform his favourite party piece. A chap next to him had just bought a glass of whisky when Cha challenged him that he could drink it without being seen. After a bit of banter the challenge had turned into a bet for fifty pence when Cha lifted that glass and downed the whisky in one gulp. Everyone watching said that was a stupid bet and they had seen him drink it. So Cha handed over the fifty pence and slyly enquired where else could he buy whisky at that price!

I also remember a year when a chancer bought quite a number of tups and collected a substantial amount of cash in luck pennies from the various sellers. At the end of the day, the tups he had bought were never paid for and they were left uncollected in their various marquees. Presumably the scam was to finance a wild night on the town but it left a sour taste with the auctioneers.

Kelso tends to sell average-priced tups to commercial farmers like myself, but there are other sales where prices can go through the roof. The record price is currently £128,100 for a five-month-old Texel ram lamb that was sold to a syndicate of breeders through Lanark auction in August 2003.

Many hard-up sheep farmers think such deals give a false impression. How can we argue the need for subsidies at a time when some will pay a small fortune for a lamb with no proven breeding record?

Such deals aren't uncommon in the sheep-breeding world, but fortunately they belong to a minority who don't live in the same world as the rest of us. It seems madness, so I will try to explain how farmers breeding top-class tups justify such high prices. Often very little money actually changes hands. A top breeder will sell two or three of his best for, say, £20,000 apiece and then buy two or three replacements for about the same.

Hill breeds like the Scottish blackface, Cheviot and Swaledale have to live in some of the harshest environments in Europe. It takes a special type of sheep to survive on high, windswept hills in a long, dreich winter. So we all need to breed hardy, good-bodied sheep with sound feet and legs, good fleeces and mothering ability.

Commercial tups for breeding such flocks can be worth up to £1,000 although some farmers I know buy them for as little as £100. The difference between a good commercial tup and a breeder's sheep is hard to define, but there is that something extra.

The buyer is looking for a bold character with cocked lugs and a glint in its eye. Good hair on head and legs as well as the correct colour markings on face and legs, which vary with fashion. That doesn't necessarily guarantee sheep that will produce lamb the public wants to eat, but these breeders are at the pinnacle of their trade. Their stock is renowned for breeding true to type and their tups will put extra quality into a commercial flock.

For a really outstanding tup, top breeders pool their resources to make sure they retain the top bloodlines. Top tups should go on to breed commercial tups that will ultimately breed tens of thousands of lambs and could have a real and lasting impact on the breed. It's just a pity such pricey deals aren't clinched privately. Little wonder that Joe Public believes we farmers are simply rolling in money!

It's almost frightening how the seasons come and go, and time quickly passes by, as you grow older. The gloriously hot, sunny summer that year almost imperceptibly gave way to a mellow, misty autumn and once again the tupping season was upon us. It's the time of year when the tups get their annual ration of passion and many of us regard that as the start of the farming year.

It's like an arable farmer sowing seed in the spring, except that the seed sheep farmers sow at tup time grows into a crop of lambs the following spring. It's certainly a very important time, because that is when the size of the lamb crop is determined.

Well-fed, thriving ewes are more likely to have twins. To encourage that we put them onto better grazing to flush them, as we call it. Mind you, ewes that carry twins or triplets don't always end up rearing them all. Fifteen per cent of all lambs born alive perish within a few days of birth. Weather conditions at lambing time are equally important.

With a gestation or pregnancy lasting twenty-one weeks, tupping is normally timed so that lambing coincides with kinder weather and the onset of spring growth. Spring grass ensures the ewe has plenty of nutritious milk for her lambs.

Twenty-one weeks are five days short of five months, so an easy way to calculate the lambing date is to deduct five days from the service date. Unlike cows, ewes don't vary their gestation by more than a couple of days, so a ewe served on the tenth of November will probably lamb on the fifth of April. Farmers use that predictability to their advantage.

Some fix a leather harness that holds a pad of chalk, or crayon as we call it, round the chests of their tups. It sits firmly against their brisket between their front legs. Such equipment is called a sire-sine harness and when the tup serves a ewe it rubs that crayon against the rump of the ewe leaving a colourful patch on the wool. By changing the colour of the crayon every week you can identify which batch of ewes is due to lamb that week in the future.

When the weather turns nasty, you can draw off those ewes that are due to lamb and put them in a sheltered field or inside a lambing shed. You would be amazed how many lambs are saved from perishing in cold, wet weather by that simple technique.

Sire-sine harnesses can also alert a farmer to infertile tups by simply changing the colour at the end of seventeen days, which is the length of a ewe's oestrus cycle. When you see ewes being marked with a different colour you know they haven't held to the first service.

Ewes are only half the flock; the other half are tups. For at least a couple of months in the run-up to tupping they are pampered with the best of feed to build them up for their season of passion. They are expected to tup at least thirty-five ewes in a seventeen-day period.

Running round a flock seeking out those ewes in season and then mating at least twice a day takes a lot out of tups. Biggest problem is they have little time to graze and they soon lose a lot of weight. Another big problem is keeping their feet sound. Lame tups soon lose interest in ewes and prefer to lie at the back of a dyke. Lameness is a big problem in sheep and a week spent trimming sheep's feet leaves me with a very sore back.

After trimming, we used to spray the hooves with an antibiotic aerosol spray. The stuff was an absolute, purple scunner and almost impossible to wash off your hands. It wasn't uncommon to see a farmer with a telltale purple thumb or index finger in the autumn.

I remember years ago a bunch of us caught a young farmer at his stag night and sprayed the soles of his feet with the stuff. You can imagine the strange looks he must have got as he lay on the beach on his honeymoon!

Once a batch of sheep has had their feet sorted we run them regularly through a footbath. Some farmers use a solution of formalin, but I prefer to use zinc sulphate, which I find has a gentler action.

There is one golden rule whilst all this preparation goes on and that is to keep the tups and ewes separate. It's that isolation that builds up tension in the tups. Fighting and head-butting are a risk at this critical period and deaths from broken necks or damaged heads are not uncommon.

The risk of a tup breaking out amongst the ewes increases, as does the risk of a ewe breaking in amongst the tups. I well remember one particularly lovesick blackie ewe that jumped the dyke into the tup field. The incident was long forgotten until one wet, dismal morning in the middle of February when a ewe was missing from the morning feed. A search of the hill was made and I found her sheltering by the bank of a burn with a newborn pair of lambs, far too early for the weather. One lamb was a white Leicester cross and the other a black, distinctly Suffolk cross as a result of her night on the tiles in late September.

She was one of the lucky ones as she and her strange twins survived. Many others in her situation would have lambed on a wild stormy night or in a heavy snowfall and probably lost her lambs from hypothermia.

Higher hill-farms than mine lamb in late April or early May and their tups are put out towards the end of November. Unlike my farm, most of the high hill-farms are unfenced and the sheep appear to wander about at will. I say 'appear', because nothing could be further from the truth.

If sheep were allowed to graze willy-nilly, there would be no way of controlling the grazings or managing a breeding programme. Tups could end up mating with their mothers and daughters. To overcome that problem, most hill ewes are hefted. A heft is a family group of sheep that can extend to hundreds. They graze a defined piece of land. It may be bounded by a road, a glen, skyline or loch and can extend to hundreds of acres.

Over the years, shepherds have worked out the optimum number of ewes to graze their hefts and herd any strays back daily. After the entire flock or hirsel has been gathered for routine tasks like shearing or dipping, each group of sheep returns to its own heft like a flight of homing pigeons. The system allows breeding programmes to be developed where tups can be rotated round the hefts. To help us identify any strays each heft has a distinct mark on their fleeces.

James Hogg, the Ettrick shepherd – writing in the eighteenth century – tells one true and well-authenticated story that testifies to the homing instincts of hefted hill sheep. A bunch of ewes had been sold and shepherded along drove roads from Harehope, the hill farm of their birth overlooking the river Tweed in the Scottish Borders, to Glen Lyon in Perthshire.

One of them – a black ewe that was nursing a lamb – strayed from her new farm and returned to her home farm, a journey that took her nine days. When he discovered she was missing, the shepherd followed her all the way to Crieff, but failed to catch up with her and returned home.

She was later seen by hundreds of people, resting on the grass by the roadside at Stirling. That was the day of Stirling's annual fair and she had decided not to proceed through the crowded streets with her lamb. She couldn't make a detour and had to go back over the trail she had followed north. Next day, at daybreak she was seen quietly stealing through the town.

The farmer at Harehope admired her so much for her amazing feat that he refunded the Highland farmer his money and kept her. She eventually died on her native heft in her seventeenth year. The hefting instinct had been so strong she had travelled nearly two hundred miles to return to the hill she was born on.

There are so many great tales from the old droving days. This was brought home to me by an old worthy I met at a market one day. 'Young ones are aye in a rush', he said with feeling. I had been complaining that the lorry transporting my cattle to market that day was late and he had overheard me. He had worked on farms all his life and passed his retirement going to markets and blethering. In his younger days he regularly drove stock on foot ten or twelve miles to the station to be transported by rail to the market.

One farmer he worked for rented a couple of farms that were ten miles apart. In the spring, cattle were driven across country, much of it open hill, to the hill farm where they spent the summer. That task took them all day. At the end of the journey the men had to walk all the way back. 'All because the farmer was too mean to hire a lorry', he quipped.

His tales of passing through small villages with a herd of cattle had us in stitches as he described how the wives had to shoo them off their gardens with brushes. One heifer once ran into a draper's shop through an open doorway and got stuck behind the counter. 'Aye, the shop was an awfy mess by the time we got her out', he added.

All of Scotland's stock was moved on foot at one time and long journeys were undertaken along the now disused drove roads. Thank goodness we now have lorries!

WINTER

8

Bringing in the beasts

Although the farm buildings were virtually derelict when I first took over the farm, I managed to adapt them to accommodate about eighty young cattle. That left about seventy cows and the breeding replacements without a roof over their heads and they had to spend the winter outside.

Not all of Scotland's cattle are in-wintered. Hardy hill-breeds like the Highlander, Galloway, Luing and their crosses do just as well outside. Over the generations they've been bred to withstand our dreich winters. These breeds, with their shaggy winter coats and natural ability to find shelter, can cope easily with the worst of weather. Even the fine-coated, Angus-cross Friesian cows that I started with, did fairly well as long as they had plenty of hay and straw supplemented with a cereal-based concentrate.

Snag with out-wintered cattle is the mess they make trampling wet land into mud and destroying pasture. Often the areas where they were fed had to be harrowed in the spring and sown with grass seeds otherwise they would simply grow a mass of thistles.

Cows on rougher hill land eat off the better grass that ewes depend on, as well as destroying fragile heather through a combination of grazing, trampling and competition from seeds that germinate where hay is scattered on the ground.

Although cattle can thrive outdoors there are other snags.

Biggest problem of all is that farmers themselves don't thrive as well outdoors in a bad winter.

Feeding cattle outside can be a very unpleasant task. Soaking wet and struggling to feed hungry cattle at the troughs can be almost impossible. Despite heaving wellington boots out of the sticky, knee-deep mud you still have to be nimble enough to keep ahead of the hungry herd that jostles for position as you put the feed into the troughs. Many are the times I have been knocked over into the muck by hungry cows.

There's also the misery of striding out into the driving rain or sleet to fetch beasts from their sheltered corner. If one of them takes ill, there's the hassle of somehow getting it to the shelter of the farm buildings to be nursed back to health.

All kinds of things can go wrong on a hill when cattle are out-wintered. I well remember a calf that was missing one morning. A search of the hill eventually found him stuck fast in a deep, mucky hole in a peat bog. All that could be seen above the waterline was his head and back. To make matters worse, the surrounding area was so boggy it was impossible to get vehicles near to pull him out.

Cha and Big Tam were summoned for help. First task was to fit a halter to the calf's head and try to ease him out. Gentle pulling persuaded him to attempt to struggle free and we managed to secure a rope to one of his front legs. After more pulling we secured his other front leg and that allowed us to begin the mighty tug of war that eventually dragged him free.

All that huffing and puffing had agitated the calf and he was in no mood to let us remove the ropes. A two-hundred-kilo beef calf takes a fair amount of manpower to restrain and the end result was that we all got thoroughly plastered in slimy peat. Once freed of his ropes the calf raced across the hill to join the rest of the cattle while we went home with a lot of dirty washing between us.

I remember the incident well because my wife's washing

machine broke down as a result of it. A quick examination revealed that the pump was jammed with a couple of washers. That's quite a common fault with our machine, as it has to wash my working clothes almost every day. On that occasion I had stripped off in a hurry and didn't empty my pockets properly, which of course can be fatal for a washing machine.

A farmer's pockets are full of bent nails, washers, nuts and bolts and all kind of odds and ends. The nails and pieces of wire are handy replacements for broken or missing split pins. When I am repairing machinery, the small nuts and bolts that didn't fit always end up in my pockets. Those bits and pieces of hardware are only a small selection of what is stored away in my various pockets.

There are also delivery notes, invoices and the leaflets that accompany medicines. None of these items wash well and when they do get washed there is usually a heated argument with my wife about who was to blame.

In other pockets you will always find my razor-sharp penknife without which all farmers are lost, but it's in the pockets of my wax-proof jacket that you will find the real treasures. A large, retracting wax crayon for marking sheep that have been ill and treated with medicines. A small shifting spanner snuggles next to ballcock spare parts and a roll of plumber's tape so I can deal with leaking water troughs immediately. Then there's the plastic syringe, with its needle safely stored in the handle, as well as some tablets for treating calves, sealed in silver foil. Elsewhere you will find three or four plastic ear tags I have found lying in the fields.

Common to most of my pockets are oily rags, dirty hankies that look like oily rags and baler twine. Without baler twine most farm repairs are impossible and engineering with twine is a technique that has been perfected by farmers.

In most pockets you will find toffees and mints although many have become detached from their wrappers and are coated in seeds and fluff. When I am about to enjoy such unlikely looking treats

I always remember 'tae spit oot the first sook so it will taste as guid as ony ither'.

My pockets are packed with a myriad of oddments although there's one item you never find. Like the Queen, I never carry money. After all, there's nothing to spend it on in the middle of a farm.

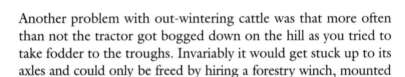

Another problem with out-wintering cattle was that more often than not the tractor got bogged down on the hill as you tried to take fodder to the troughs. Invariably it would get stuck up to its axles and could only be freed by hiring a forestry winch, mounted on the back of a big, four-wheel-drive tractor.

Then there was the problem of getting to the cattle after a blizzard. Every gateway would be blocked with snowdrifts that had to be dug through. It took me five years to finance the building of the big shed that houses my cattle and, although it was a major investment, it is one that I have never regretted.

Nowadays the herd calves in two batches. The first half calve indoors in February and March and the rest calve in May and June outside at grass. I often bring the cattle into the sheds in the middle of October, although a mild, open autumn might tempt me to leave them out until the beginning of November. Many years I could leave them outside a little longer, but experience has taught me that's a false economy.

There may appear to be enough grass on the hill and the cows' stomachs may well be full, but they will start to roar for feeding whenever they hear a tractor. Grass at that time of the year has a low nutritional value and the cows sense it. They may look fine, but often they will have stopped putting on weight. In fact, the feeding value of the grass may be such that they can actually lose weight.

It costs a lot to put beef back onto cattle once they're indoors and on expensive rations, so the best policy is to bring them in before they lose any weight. Another disadvantage of leaving cattle outside too long in the autumn is that they will start growing their thick, hairy, winter coats. So when they're brought indoors, they sweat and don't thrive so well.

But the main reason for bringing the cattle in is to conserve the remaining grass on the hill for sheep to winter on. An extra fortnight's grazing for cattle at that time of year could mean a month's starvation for the ewes at a time when they are heavy in lamb.

First task is to tidy away all the clutter that builds up in the cattle sheds during the summer. Then the silage pit has to be opened and that involves removing several hundred old tyres, before rolling back the plastic sheet the tyres had been keeping secure. Finally, gates have to be set up to guide the cattle into their winter quarters.

The secret of success is to have plenty of troops to lend a hand. Not that my cattle are wild or difficult to work with, but young calves can panic at the sight of the buildings and bolt. Beef calves easily outrun farmers and their assistants so it's always best to prevent such incidents by having plenty of people on hand.

The first time we brought the cattle into the newly finished shed it was a beautiful clear November morning with just a bite of coldness in the wind. A couple of blackcock whisked silently away to safety as we approached, the sun glinting off their backs. A hill hare, just starting to turn white, paused to watch us out of curiosity. But amid all this peace and tranquillity there were no coos!

My Limousin bull, Jimmy to the children, had smashed an ancient gate while relieving an awkward itch against it. The herd had escaped, or rather vanished, into a two-hundred-acre plantation of half-grown conifers.

We could hear them roaring to each other amongst the trees, but could we see them?

While the cattle seemed to enjoy charging through the trees with us in mad pursuit, we found the constant whiplash of fir branches in our faces pure hell. After much sweating, bruising, scratching and more than a few curses, the wayward herd was driven back out onto open hill ground.

Then, to our horror, we noticed the next problem. One of the wildest cows in the herd had a snare firmly secured to her ankle. Madam had managed to put her hoof into it and break it free of its securing post. Enraged, she kept running off from the herd and doubling back on us, much to the annoyance of the rest of us who had to keep sprinting through peat and over sheep drains to head her off.

Cha is one of those unusual athletes who trains on a strict diet of fish suppers and Chinese carry-outs, washed down by copious quantities of beer. He is virtually a chain smoker yet, despite all that, he's genuinely one of the fastest, fittest men I know and was by far the closest to the runaway. Eventually a mighty roar came from Cha, 'It's aff!' The suction of wet peat had drawn the snare off of her leg as she ran through wet, boggy ground. With the snare off, the cow calmed down and meekly trotted off the hill and into the shed with the rest of them to be penned for the winter.

Once the first batch of thirty-five older calves that were born in February and March are safely indoors, we separate them from their mothers to wean, or spean, them. The second batch of about thirty younger calves that were born in May and June are too young to spean. To allow them to continue suckling their mothers they have to be penned together in small groups of about a dozen.

Nowadays, when the calves are born, I fix two official ear tags that are required by law as well as a large management tag. I simply write the cow's number, with special plastic ink, onto that plastic management-tag. That way I know which calves belong to which cows.

The only snag with that system is that cattle start to grow their hairy winter coats at that time of year. The hairiest part of a beast is often its lugs and a bunch of hair hangs down to cover the number on the ear tag. After much squinting and peering, the cattle are eventually identified and drawn into their lots. There are always a few sleepless nights as the cattle settle into the winter quarters. Until they do, young calves roar out to their mothers while the cows bellow back to reassure their youngsters.

Once indoors for the winter, bored cattle get up to all kinds of tricks. If they aren't lying down or eating they are sniffing, licking, chewing or rubbing. Their favourite trick is to knock the cover off the water trough ballcock while rubbing their itchy heads. Then it's simply a matter of licking the plastic ball on the ballcock with their rough tongues until it unscrews and floats uselessly in the trough. Imagine my mood at finding a flooded pen next morning!

In my main cattle shed the feed is placed in a passageway that has a row of pens on either side. Cattle are kept in their pens and prevented from trampling the feed by feed barriers that are designed so that they can poke their heads through to eat.

Another favourite trick is to knock out the pins that fasten the feed barriers in place. I tie them with string to stop that happening, but the cattle undo the knots by a combination of licking and chewing. A quick dunt with their head is all it takes to knock the pen out. That allows them to escape onto the feed passage for frolics and wacky races. Guess who sweeps up the mucky passage afterwards?

I remember one stunt that old Jimmy the bull pulled off. He loved rubbing his itchy head against the alkathene water pipe supplying his drinking bowl and making a rattling sound that fascinated him. But constantly rubbing against the rough wall wore away the pipe causing it to leak and soak his straw-bedded pen. I had to fit a cover plate to protect the pipe.

Itchiness is a real problem. Some farmers fit big brushes onto special frames at the right height for the cattle. Beasts use it to give their sides and backs a really good, itch-relieving rub. That also saves wear and tear on the pens and keeps them out of mischief.

Once they have been indoors for a week or so and have settled down, I set up a hairdressing salon so the young cattle can have a short back and sides. The shaggy winter coat they started to grow before they came in becomes a handicap, particularly in a mild autumn when the sheds become hot and humid. That causes the cattle to sweat and uncomfortable cattle don't thrive properly.

Best solution is to shave their heads and a strip along their backs with a set of cattle clippers. About 80 per cent of their body heat is lost that way, so a good trim cools the beasts down. It's like taking your bonnet off when you're hot.

First task is to put each beast into a cattle crush. It's a strong metal crate, a bit longer and higher than a cow. At the front of the crush is a sliding bar that closes, not too tightly, on the animal's neck to stop it pulling its head back and trying to turn round. At the back is a strong metal gate that slams into place as soon as the animal is in and stops it backing out.

It's all easier said than done. On big farms – handling hundreds of cattle – there is usually a permanent cattle crush, fixed firmly in place with a narrow passage, or race, the width of a cow leading into it. Once into that race the beast has no option but to go straight ahead.

On an average farm, and I am the first to admit I am average, the crush is taken to where it's needed. Instead of a strong narrow race, I make a temporary one and a pen using metal gates and lots of string. It's not ideal, but most of the time it works. The cattle know me and I try never to rush things and get them excited.

Given time, most of them will go into the crush to be clipped, dosed for stomach worms or vaccinated, as well as blood-tested by the vet. Now and again a headbanger comes along. A cow or bullock that doesn't like to be touched and that definitely doesn't like the look of a big metal crush with no way out.

Some reckon that a few of the Continental breeds we have imported in the last thirty years can be the worst but I reckon a Galloway takes a bit of beating. They are one of our native hill breeds with shaggy black coats that can be as wild as the heather they were reared on.

I once saw one go into the crush at fifty miles an hour! She hit the catching mechanism at full speed and charged off into the distance with bits of it round her neck. Thankfully I wasn't standing in front of it waiting to read her ear tag when she hurtled through.

Others are the exact opposite and become immovable. Cattle often associate the crush with vets taking blood samples and giving them vaccinations.

Like kids going for a routine jab, the thought of needles terrifies them even though they seldom notice when the task is done. It's not easy trying to push a reluctant, half-ton beast into a crush. They dig their heels in and stand there whilst you turn blue in the face and start to pant. A good trick in such cases is to get someone to open the front of the crush to give the beast the impression it can walk through and then close it once it's in.

Once they are caught in the crush they needlessly wriggle and writhe as I harmlessly shave a strip, about four inches wide, along the centre of their backs. Some go berserk when you start to shave their heads but patience always wins the day and they soon realise it's all quite painless.

Nowadays I pour a measured amount of wormer along their backs that's absorbed through the skin and eventually kills stomach worms as well as lice. Lice can be a real problem in sheds during the winter, making cattle constantly rub their itchy heads against feed barriers and gate posts, Their heads also get mucky as they scratch the back of their ears with their hind hooves. Clipping also helps to tidy them up although there are occasional small tufts of hair left. Fortunately the difference between a good haircut and a bad one is only about a fortnight.

My herd is relatively disease-free since it became a closed one back in 1991. A closed herd is one that breeds its own replacements and the only new cattle I introduce are bulls that are carefully quarantined beforehand. My system is now based on using a Beef Shorthorn to breed replacement females and then crossing them with the Aberdeen Angus. Each generation is crossed alternately with either the Shorthorn or Angus in order to maintain hybrid vigour in the herd.

Although Continental-bred beef is leaner than beef from our traditional breeds, it isn't as succulent. Traditional British breeds were developed to convert grass into cheap, tender beef. Such beef has fine textured meat with a marbling of fat, allowing it to retain flavour and moisture during cooking. Many butchers now recognise this and pay a premium for traditional beasts. You still can't whack an Aberdeen Angus steak.

I remember as a boy being at the Perth bull sales with my father in 1963, when Sir Torquil Munro of Lindertis farm, Kirriemuir sold Lindertis Evulse for 60,000 guineas. That price set a British record for the breed that has never been broken. The bull was bought on behalf of a syndicate of investors from America. They owned Blackwatch Farms in New York state and imported him to mate with their pedigree herd.

Unfortunately, he proved to be infertile and was slaughtered. Lindertis Evulse ended up as the most expensive mince that the world has ever known!

Fashions change, and after American ranchers in Stetsons disappeared from the Perth bull sales, the breed went through thirty years of decline. There has been an upsurge of interest in the Aberdeen Angus again because it is a thrifty one that doesn't need a lot of expensive feeding.

As my grandfather often said, 'Farmers shouldn't keep cows, it's the cow's job to keep the farmer.'

9

Those wonderful country smells

Animals have a very keen sense of smell and they need to, as their eyesight isn't as good as our own. They rely on their noses as well as their ears to warn of predators approaching.

Deer, hares and rabbits constantly sniff the air as they graze and they'll often smell a human long before you can spot their camouflaged forms on the hillside. Smell is also used in the animal world to mark out territory and, of course, cattle and sheep identify their young by scent.

Sadly our own sense of smell has all but vanished and a scent has to be really strong for us to notice it. Certain scents are unforgettable, like the smell of a fox. Its strange, musky odour seems to linger in the air and is almost as strong as the smell of a smoker.

Pigs, cattle, sheep and hens all have distinctive smells and while some of them may be strong, I believe none are offensive. Stockmen often carry the smell of the beasts they work with, just as there's a whiff of diesel and grease about tractormen and dairymen reek of the chemicals they use to clean milking equipment.

Mind you, there's one smell most townsfolk find unpleasant and that's the smell of silage. As I explained earlier it's basically pickled grass, but it can be very smelly. Most farmers enjoy the sharp tang of well-made silage, but it does cling to boiler suits, wellingtons and overcoats. My wife doesn't allow my working clothes past the back lobby during the winter months when I am feeding silage to the cattle. That way she keeps the smell out of the house.

Like a smoker who doesn't know he smells of cigarette smoke, I don't realise that I reek of silage. That point was brought home to me once as I queued in the newspaper shop. A wee lassie was holding her nose when she explained loudly, 'Mummy, there's an awful smell of sickness.' Imagine my embarrassment when the shopkeeper explained to me later that I was the root cause of the problem.

There are other smells on a farm and dung is probably one of the more noticeable. Strangely, I don't find the smell of dung unpleasant and most country folk will say the same. Poultry muck has a strong ammonia type of smell, while that from pigs is unmistakable if you ever drive past a piggery that's being cleaned out. Dairy cow slurry – a mix of dung, water and urine – has a sharp smell compared with the pleasanter smell of an outside muck midden.

Sadly the finer points of dung, muck and slurry aromas are lost on my wife. All day long the farmhouse windows and doors are kept tightly shut and she continually moans about the smell when we are spreading.

Farm dung is handled in two forms, slurry or muck. Slurry, as I said, is made up of dung, water and urine that has been mechanically mixed for storage. It's a thick liquid and is sprayed onto the land with tractor-drawn slurry tankers. It's the stuff that leaves a real whiff in the air and is usually produced by dairy herds and piggeries.

Muck on the other hand is produced in straw-bedded cattle sheds and is a mixture of straw and dung. At one time muck was stored in a three-walled midden in the farmyard that gradually filled up during the winter. Barrowloads of dung, shovelled from the byre, were carefully wheeled up the slippery, steep and narrow wooden plank that climbed up the ever-growing midden and tipped. This was a skilful art that took a fair amount of practice. Failure to get it right ended in a headlong dive into soggy, smelly dark-brown stuff!

In the spring, after the cattle have been turned out to grass, I muck out the sheds that were bedded with straw. It's stacked in a heap or temporary midden at the edge of the field it is going to be spread on.

Throughout the summer, bacterial activity gradually composts the heap so that it is ready to spread on the stubble fields in the autumn. Raw muck needs to be composted to break it down to a consistency that's easy to spread mechanically. Composting also generates heat that kills off the weed seeds present in bedding straw. One of the snags with slurry is that – as it is stored in liquid form – it doesn't compost, and seeds from weeds like dockens in the hay and silage can survive. Such weeds are now a real problem in modern grassland.

By returning muck or slurry to the land, we replenish the nutrients that were used to grow the barley crop.

I well remember the backbreaking job of mucking out by hand. The tangled muck was torn out with hacks, a type of fork with the prongs at right angles to the wooden shaft. Then it was passed back by forks, or graips as we call them in Scotland, to the doorway where it was eventually loaded onto trailers.

Hydraulic fore-loaders changed all that once the doorways had been widened to allow the tractor into the old-fashioned buildings. That involved removing masses of rubble, because the walls were thirty inches thick and made from stone and mortar. After that I installed new lintels and doors, until all the old buildings with narrow doors were converted and graiping became a task of the past. Modern sheds are obviously designed to allow ready tractor access, so that both feed and muck can be handled with ease.

There is still one snag with a fore-loader and that is that no matter how carefully you drive, some muck falls off the mechanical fork while other bits fall off the side of the trailer. So a graip is still needed to clean up the mess.

Once the harvest was safely gathered in, the fields were gleaned of any grain left on the ground by partridges, pheasants, crows and pigeons. Later, in the gloaming, mallard ducks would fly in for an evening feed on any gleanings left by the daytime scavengers. After that, those golden stubbles were spread with muck before ploughing started in late autumn. That allows the winter's frosts to break down the cloddy earth making the soil easy to work in the spring.

Ploughing was always reckoned to be the most important job on the farm. It was a new beginning for the land!

Many areas had ancient traditions celebrating the start of the ploughing season. In the north-east of Scotland, the cutting of the first furrow used to be marked by the farmer's wife offering food and refreshment to the ploughman. As she handed over the meal she would command 'guid speed the wark', to which he solemnly replied 'guid speed it'. He then sat on the plough's beam and ate the simple ploughman's lunch while his Clydesdale horses waited patiently.

Good ploughmen take a pride in their work and there are many ploughing matches where competitors draw lots for a piece of land to prove their skills in front of critical judges. There are many different classes, like ploughing with horses, vintage tractors or massive modern tractors with sophisticated ploughs. Skilled ploughmen can aspire to winning the world championship.

Ploughing is one of the most basic, as well as one of the most highly skilled, tasks in farming. At one time the ploughman relied on his pair of heavy horses to pull together as a team. A wonderful bond of understanding built up between the ploughman and his horses, which were usually Clydesdales. At the end of a hard day those horses had to be stabled and fed. Next day's work got under way long before daybreak, with the ploughman tending to his horses before harnessing them up for another long, hard day.

The modern ploughman's task may not be so hard physically, but it requires just as much skill. Today's giant tractors can have the power of more than a hundred horses under their bonnet but all that horsepower needs just as much attention as a pair of Clydesdales. Tractors have to be regularly and properly serviced and refuelled.

The problem with ploughs is that they wear away and every year there are worn parts to be replaced. Sadly, the nuts become worn as well, making it impossible to grip them properly with a spanner, so they have to be removed with a hammer and chisel. On a freezing cold winter's day such tools can be lethal weapons as my skinned and bruised knuckles used to testify.

So today's ploughmen may not have the drudgery of our grandfather's generation, but their job is just as demanding. What isn't in question is that it's a lot lonelier. At least our grandfathers had their horses to talk to and their fellow workers for company at meal breaks.

A furrow is a strip of land about fourteen inches wide that is turned upside down by the plough. The idea is to bury all the turf, trash and weed seeds and expose fresh soil that becomes a seedbed. That also helps mix the soil and improves drainage, but it's not as easy as it looks.

The plough has to be kept at a constant depth and not allowed to bring up infertile subsoil. Most farmers aim to plough at a depth of about eight or ten inches depending on the type of land and crops to be grown. All of the trash on the surface must be buried out of sight. Above all else you must plough a furrow as straight as an arrow shot from a bow.

Snag is, you spend most of your time looking backwards and making minor adjustments to the various controls on the plough. It goes without saying that less-skilled ploughmen like myself often end up with squiggly furrows, or full of dog's legs as my father used to say. Skilled ploughmen delight in fiddling with the various adjustments ön both tractor and plough so that even-sized furrows are turned over neatly.

Years ago only the most experienced horsemen were allowed to plough. In Orkney they trained young men to plough on the sandy beaches. That way, any bad ploughing was washed from sight by the incoming tide.

My training wasn't so easy, as the farm where I grew up was very stony. As the plough slid around or over a stone it was guaranteed to make a dog's leg of the furrow. Worse was the fact that there were no level fields and they were full of uneven humps or knowes. One minute you were ploughing a knowe that sloped steeply to the left only to find that the next one fell away to the right. No matter how I adjusted the plough, I always ended up off the straight and narrow.

My untidy work then lay exposed for all the neighbours and passers-by to laugh at. No wonder I was glad to harrow the fields in the spring to level down and cover up my embarrassment.

It's amazing the variation in soil that can exist in a single field. There can be wet patches of heavy clay in the hollows, or thin gravelly stuff on the knowes. There's an old saying that you don't know your farm till you have ploughed it.

Each different type of soil has different levels of fertility. The best parts of my fields are rich in worms while the cold, wet, clay patches have virtually none. The best indicators of where the fertile parts lie are the seagulls and crows that feed hungrily on the worms and grubs that the plough turns up. Those feathered companions can help to break the day's monotony. It's not uncommon for an eager, hungry gull to get too close to the plough and become trapped between two furrows. The sight of their head sticking out from between two furrows as they squawk indignantly always makes me laugh, although often their only thanks when you release them is a peck on the hand.

Another break in a monotonous day can be the unpleasant fright of a low-flying jet. It's a horrible experience to be startled by a jet when you're out on a tractor, and the unexpected sonic boom they create makes me jump out of my skin.

Even worse is the irrational thought that the bang is the engine blowing up or the gearbox disintegrating. Only when I see the black reek across the sky do I realise that once again I have been supersonically surprised. That's when I brace myself for the next one, as they always seem to train in pairs.

Low-flying jets are common where I live as the surrounding hills and glens make ideal terrain for training. Perhaps the biggest attraction is that our area is sparsely populated and fewer folk mean fewer complaints.

As a toddler, my younger daughter used to be terrified of such planes. Many are the times we have found her sobbing beneath her bed or hiding under a blackcurrant bush in the garden.

Farm animals don't take kindly to low-flying jets either. Startled calves run panic stricken across the fields causing their cows to stampede. Frightened cattle injure themselves jumping out of their pens in the sheds and newly born lambs run in terror from their ewes.

Perhaps the most frustrating time is when a low-flying jet passes over, just when you are moving livestock. Collie dogs dash off and cower under a hedge or dyke allowing the animals to stampede so that the job has to be abandoned until everything calms down.

Listening to the chorus of startled birds and livestock, I can't help but think that shattering the countryside peace in this manner is a sacrilege.

Mind you, there are strict rules for the pilots to ignore. They aren't allowed to fly below two hundred feet, although that rule is regularly broken. Many are the times I have stood on a hillside and watched a jet fly through the glen below me. I have also watched them climb steeply to avoid a hilltop and only just clear it.

RAF procedure for reporting jets that fly too low is daft. You are supposed to note the jet's number and the time of the incident. How are you supposed to read the number of a jet that is travelling faster than sound? By the time you have recovered your wits it's miles away. Reporting an incident results in 'the matter being investigated', which is official jargon for 'so what?'

Sometimes the weather turns so wet you simply can't plough. It's not so much that tractor wheels can't get a proper grip in the greasy land, because modern four-wheel-drive tractors are capable of ploughing uphill on a glacier and can plough all but the wettest land. Biggest risk in wet weather is that the earth gets compacted and irreparably damages the soil structure.

Another downside is that heavy tractors, once bogged, can damage drainage systems when freeing themselves. There's also the real risk of creating a plough pan. That's where the smearing action of the ploughshares cutting through the wet soil forms an impervious layer about ten inches below ground, particularly in heavy clays. A plough pan hinders drainage and creates a barrier that roots find hard to penetrate.

So it's always best to wait till the land dries out before ploughing. That's a real test of patience. If you wait too long, there might not be enough time to plough, then cultivate the seedbeds and get the crops sown on time.

My main memories of ploughing, before heated cabs came on the scene, are of the bitter cold. In the evening as I stiffly stepped down from the tractor I was sometimes never sure if my toes were still connected to my feet. No matter how many layers of clothing I wore, my hands and feet often felt like blocks of ice. Many are the times I have clasped the tractor exhaust to warm my frozen hands.

Typical garb for such work included vests, heavy cotton shirts, pullovers, heavy trousers, boiler suits, leggings, tweed jacket and a heavy army overcoat. Then there were scarves, gloves and a woolly balaclava hat.

I have been wearing balaclavas for as long as I can remember. As a wellie-wearing toddler splashing about in muddy puddles in the yard I wore mother's hand-knitted versions. Later as a fashion-conscious teenager, I became acutely aware they were soppy looking. That's when I was first treated to a proper one like my dad's.

Bought from an outdoor clothing shop, they're tightly knit and have a slightly fluffy finish on the outside. When it's raining, water sits on the hat rather than penetrating and soaking it. As long as you regularly shake the water off, you can keep it dry in all but the worst rain. Even when it's soaked, it keeps you warm because wet wool warms up, which is why deerstalkers and game-keepers prefer woolly tweeds.

Balaclavas folded up are an ideal bonnet. As soon as it starts to rain, or when a keen wind gets up, you simply pull it down over your lugs. About 80 per cent of our body heat can be lost through the head, so it's important to keep it snug.

Balaclavas, like other bonnets, have many uses. When sheep or cattle look like turning the wrong way, you throw it in front of them and that's often enough to change their direction. Many are the times a clutch of hen eggs was safely carried home in my bal-aclava. Some folk use their bonnet to vent their anger. My father often threw his to the ground when in a rage.

They also make a social statement. Factors, bankers and estate agents tend to wear trendy tweed caps while shepherds and game-keepers often prefer the deerstalker type and tractormen and dairymen wear woolly bonnets. As for me, I am unique, as I am the only one in these parts with a balaclava. So what! Someone has to set new trends in farmer fashions.

My biggest breakthrough in keeping warm whilst ploughing was when an old timer suggested I wear a pair of my wife's tights. They certainly kept my legs warm although I never dared mention it to Cha and Big Tam.

Ploughing also gives me the opportunity to gather worms that I bait with the deadly poison strychnine to kill moles, or moudies as we call them. I used to give each bairn a bucket to fill and they loved every minute of it, often squabbling over which one had found the biggest.

Moudie hills are a real nuisance and the small stones in them can cause expensive breakdowns with mowers and silage-making equipment. Soil from those little moudie hills contaminates silage and leads to a fatal disease in sheep called listeriosis. So it's important to control moudies in the winter months while they are tunnelling actively allowing you to see where they are working.

Few of us have the time to check traps daily so most of us use strychnine under licences granted after attending a short course on how to use it. The technique involves sprinkling small amounts of the poison on worms and then placing the deadly bait in moudie runs.

A favourite run to bait is the one that leads to water, because moudies have to drink regularly. They aren't always as easy to find as the main runs that are found close to dykes or under the bottom wire of a fence. Moudies aren't daft and tunnel their main runs where they won't get trampled by grazing cattle or sheep. That's why a fresh infestation always starts at the edge of a field.

10

'Turning a pound into tuppence'

Scotland is the greatest country in the world despite being one of Europe's most northerly and lying close to the Arctic Circle. That's grand in the summertime, as it means we get a lot more daylight than the rest of Europe. Northerly Caithness, Orkney and Shetland enjoy almost twenty-four hours of daylight and are referred to as the land of the midnight sun.

Unfortunately the nights are much longer in the winter and there is so little precious daylight that it has to be used wisely.

Dark winter mornings are a real scunner and I am always glad to see the back of the shortest day. From then on, my spirits steadily improve as the days gradually get longer. No wonder folk get SAD, or seasonal affective disorder. It's a type of depression brought on by the absence of daylight.

Farm animals are also affected by the amount of daylight. Sunshine is vital for their health and is particularly important in the production of vitamin D that helps calcium and phosphorous to be deposited in bones. Lack of vitamin D leads to rickets and can be a problem in young growing animals in the dead of winter.

Cattle don't really thrive until after the New Year when growth rates increase with the lengthening days. Wool also grows in response to daylight and grows fastest on the longest day so that sheep are guaranteed a heavy fleece to cope with the cold blasts of late autumn and winter.

Breeding cycles for many animals are triggered by the amount of daylight. In common with a lot of animals that give birth in the spring, ewes come into season in the autumn in response to shortening hours of daylight. That way their lambs are born in the spring when, it is hoped, the weather is kinder and grass is starting to grow.

Cattle and pigs, on the other hand, are reluctant to mate in the dead of winter. It's harder to spot dairy cows and outdoor sows in season in December and January and conception rates with artificial insemination are often lower in those months, compared to the spring.

Most birds mate in the spring when the days are getting longer and as a result their eggs hatch at the start of summer, when there is an abundance of insects to feed their young on.

Hens are no different and also produce most of their eggs in the spring. That used to lead to a shortage of eggs during winter, when the nights are longest. To overcome that problem, modern poultry farmers control the amount of artificial light in their laying sheds. As a result they can keep their egg supply fairly steady throughout the year.

My wife runs a small flock of free-range hens that used to lay fewer eggs during the winter. That meant she had to ration them to her customers and often had a glut around Easter. That all changed when I installed electricity in her henhouses so that a timer can be set to switch on the lights at 2 a.m. in the winter and switch them off at daybreak. That extra light fools the hens into thinking it's spring and keeps them laying eggs.

Farmers have traditionally been stout defenders of changing the clocks back in the autumn. My father was typical of many that believed that 'an hour in the morning is worth two in the afternoon.'

He loved to be up before daybreak and have a day's work done before breakfast. I remember how father hated it when the nation stopped putting the clocks back as an experiment in the sixties. He grumpily hung about the buildings till nearly nine o'clock, waiting for daylight and the chance to feed the animals outside in the fields.

Parents claimed it wasn't safe sending children to school in the dark and after three years of lobbying the government relented and we returned to the old system of changing the clocks. But I'm not so sure that it's such a good idea nowadays.

An extra hour of daylight in the afternoon would give children the chance to play outdoors after school. Businessmen would find it easier to phone customers and colleagues in the rest of Europe without having to think about the time differences and travellers wouldn't have to worry about remembering to change their watches.

It wouldn't even affect farmers much nowadays, as most of us have moved on in the past thirty years and developed sophisticated livestock buildings. With the exception of a few pigs that live outdoors on free-range systems, most pigs and poultry are kept in buildings with electric lighting.

Dairy cows are all milked before daylight in state-of-the-art, well-lit sheds and even beef cattle are now mostly kept indoors. Only sheep have to be fed outdoors and I don't think that waiting an extra hour will make much difference, as long as they are fed at the same time every morning.

In fact, an extra hour of darkness in the morning could help some modern farmers. Quite a few farmers' wives now work off the farm, so farmers often have to get the children ready for school. If that had to be done in the dark it would leave an extra hour of daylight for outside farm work. Mind you, I can still hear my father's voice ringing in my ears as he shouted upstairs, 'lying in bed all day doesn't get the work done'.

I remember an occasion when Big Tam had got caught out after his clock was put back an hour. Cha and Tam had been having a wee dram one Saturday evening. Part of the conversation had centred on a large, antique clock that hung on a wall in Tam's kitchen. He had bought it at a local auction and had lovingly restored it. According to Tam, it was the most accurate clock he had ever owned.

Later on in the evening, Cha put that clock back an hour when Tam was out of the kitchen answering the phone. You can imagine his embarrassment and confusion the next morning when he arrived late at church as the service was about to end!

Farm animals love routine and you will often see dairy cows gathering at a gateway just before milking time. They even tend to come into the milking parlour in the same order, some preferring to be milked first while others wait at the end of the queue.

It's the same with sheep. Shepherds drive their flock up the hill in the evening and down from the top in the morning so that the hill is evenly grazed. If the shepherd were to be off work for a few days, the sheep would still move up and down the hill at their usual time.

Beef cattle particularly love routine and soon settle into one after coming into the sheds for the winter. Their morning feed starts at quarter to eight and if breakfast isn't served by half-past-eight they shout the house down. A hundred and fifty cattle roaring for a bite to eat is deafening. It's the same in the afternoon when the second feed of the day has to start at three o'clock, or else!

Some of the tricks that cattle learn to get a little extra food are beyond belief. They craftily nudge the bag as you walk past them, thus knocking a bigger portion into the trough space in front of them. Others reach through the feed barrier and pull bales or silage off the trailer with their tongues as it reverses into the shed.

Christmas and New Year are working days like any other on a farm and in common with nurses, firemen and the police I have a daily routine. Cattle and sheep have to be checked, fed or bedded with straw. Only when those chores are done can I sit down to the turkey or have a dram.

I arrange the workload to be the bare minimum, about three hours, although things don't always go as smoothly as planned. Like that New Year's Day when there was a punctured silage-trailer tyre. That fairly made me curse my luck as I jacked up the trailer and tried to free those big wheel nuts. Several years of rust and muck had seized them on solid.

After half-an-hour straining, I eventually gave in and fetched the blowlamp. Heating those nuts till they were red hot expanded them enough to allow me to free them. A herd of cattle bellowing for feed in the background is a good incentive to hurry up with a repair.

Of course, there was then no way the puncture could be repaired as the local garage was closed. Fortunately the spare wheel on the Land Rover fits that particular trailer and is strong enough to do the job in an emergency.

Just as lambing time should have a known starting date, so should there also be a known and definite ending. To avoid late lambing ewes, I bring the tups in from the ewes on Auld Year's Day. That way my lambing is over by the May Term, so while others are having a nap and gathering strength for Hogmanay parties and first footing, I am out working. After bringing the tups into the wee field at the back of the house, the various lots of ewes are returned to their hill grazings.

Tupping is hard work. Constantly inspecting a harem of over fifty leaves little time for grazing, never mind rest. Once strong and proud, those tups are now thin and weary-looking and ready to be pampered in that wee field. Gradually, a diet of good meadow hay and concentrates, as well as rest, restores most of them to their former glory.

Sadly for some, January marks the end of their career. They may have become too old or been proved infertile or lethargic breeders. Others may not have developed the way they should. Whatever the reason, January is the time of year for selling unwanted or cast tups and around the country there are big sales of them.

Mutton from old tups is very strong-flavoured and it often ends up in mutton pies. It's sad to see those old gentlemen huddled together in pens waiting for their turn in the auction ring. Indeed it's hard to imagine many were sold for thousands of pounds when they were in their prime. And it seems beyond belief that some had even won trophies at shows and had their photographs featured in the farming press. Age is one of nature's greatest levellers until death finally reduces us all to the same state. No admiring glances at this auction, instead there is only a handful of dealers trying to keep warm on a cold January morning.

The problem with cast-tup sales is that they can be very cold affairs. Your feet and hands become frozen numb with the keen wind always blowing through the market at that time of year. When you are chilled through and miserable, the time it takes to wait for your turn to sell seems an eternity.

I once passed the time at such a cold sale, about fifteen years ago, talking to an elderly farmer who farmed a few miles from me. His nose had turned a bluish purple with the cold and not with drink, as he was too canny to buy the stuff. His old overcoat was tied round his waist with baler twine and his wellingtons had pink puncture-repair-patches on them.

He had brought along a couple of goats with his consignment of cast tups. Sadly he had invested in goats in the eighties when they were all the rage. The idea was to produce mohair and cashmere to sell to the luxury textile market at inflated prices. But the biggest attraction at the time was to produce breeding stock to sell at ridiculously inflated prices and six or seven thousand pounds for a buck was commonplace.

As with all such fast money-making projects, the bubble had burst and such fancy-priced animals became worth no more than twenty or thirty pounds apiece. So I asked him what he thought of goat farming.

After sucking thoughtfully on his pipe for a while he replied, 'in all my forty years of farming I have never found anything as good at turning a pound into tuppence!'

He was a hardy old man who had started out as a shepherd but, by sheer hard work, scrimping and saving every last penny and just a pinch of good luck, had ended up with one of the finest farms in the district. He had worked a full day right up to his sudden and unexpected death at seventy-eight and was sadly missed by all those who knew him.

Because he was so helpful and kind he made many friends, both young and old, from far and wide. He was never too busy to give a hand or offer advice and I always enjoyed listening to his tales of the great agricultural depression of the thirties.

His favourite saying, and one that he was fond of quoting was, 'live today as if you are going to die tomorrow, but farm as if you are going to live forever'. His point, of course, was that you should build up the fertility of your farm and quality of livestock by long-term investments.

Rural communities are very tight-knit, so when someone like him dies, the funeral can be enormous by any standards. His was as big as I have ever seen and the parish kirk was full to capacity, with maybe a hundred standing quietly outside in respect.

It had been his wish, as is common with country folk, to be buried in the parish of his birth beside his family. After the church service the cortege set off on the thirty-mile-long journey to his final resting-place. There at the graveyard stood another five hundred friends, patiently waiting to pay their last respects. A vast congregation of about fourteen hundred laid the old man to rest. Though he wasn't famous, young and old, farmworkers and lairds, stood shoulder to shoulder mourning the loss of one of their community.

As we left the graveyard I was speaking to another old worthy, a retired blacksmith, who told me they had been to school together as laddies. He reminisced how they had walked the eight-mile shortcut over the hills on a Saturday to go dancing in the nearby town. 'Aye, son', he said to me, 'it's gey worrying when He starts drawing them frae your ain pen!'

Cast-tup sales are also a good opportunity to negotiate with the dealers to buy tup horns back from the abattoir to make into crooks. Like Moses without his staff, a farmer without a stick is unthinkable. Sticks come in various shapes and sizes, from rough-looking bullock herders, just simple sticks or even lengths of plumber's alkathene pipes, to the fancy crooks we use on market day.

Although I wouldn't actually hit an animal with a stick, the sight of it being waved up and down will turn most cattle in the right direction. Separating cattle without the aid of a stick is an almost futile exercise and crooks are also essential for catching nimble sheep. Younger, athletic types can catch sheep with their bare hands, but it isn't easy and you often end up with just a handful of wool. With skill and collie dogs, however, you can entice a sheep to run past you and then catch it by the neck with the crook. Even more useful, is the amount of leverage a stick gives when climbing a steep brae, when it becomes a shepherd's third leg.

Crooks are made from a straight hazel shank and a tup's horn, and only horn from a mature tup will do. They're twisted and set into shape after gently heating over an oil lamp, as the hard horn becomes malleable when hot. Then they are filed down, fitted to the shank, carved, polished and varnished.

Some are real works of art. Thistles, collie dogs, pheasants and fish are just some of the things carved on a fancy crook. Often the farmer's name and his farm are engraved on the side.

It's hard to find good horns suitable for making into crooks as there aren't that many horned tups. Worse still, shepherds often set the growing horns on a young tup by heating them and such horns become flawed and don't make good crooks.

I used to make crooks for a hobby and have several fancy ones I show off on market days. But my main crook is the plain one I use for everyday work. Every so often it gets broken and I have to fit a new shank.

Good straight hazel shanks are almost as hard to come by as good horns. Shanks are best cut in the late autumn when all the sap has returned to the roots. They are then gently dried in a loft for a couple of years, because a shank that has not been thoroughly dried before fitting will twist and warp.

Many are the times I have kept a watchful eye on a good straight hazel shank, growing in a nearby wood, that I have earmarked as ideal for reshanking broken crooks. Often as not someone gets there before me and takes it, proving the old saying, 'you should aye cut a stick when you see it.'

A spell of frost is an important part of the farming calendar, as it kills off slugs that eat seedlings, insects that spread disease and fungi that damage crop leaves. Frost is Mother Nature's way of controlling pests and it's cheaper than chemical sprays and probably as effective. Recent mild, wet winters have allowed pests like ticks to increase in numbers, so a cold snap helps to reduce them. Frost is also necessary to break down clods in ploughed land, making it easier to work up a fine seedbed in the spring.

It's grand to be able to wear warm leather boots instead of squelching through mud in cold wellingtons. Frost is also the cook's best friend. Brussel sprouts that haven't been frosted aren't worth eating and taste far sweeter after a hard spell. It's the same with neeps and eating them before they have had a touch of frost gives me wind.

Mind you, I well remember in my youth we used to lift a cartload of neeps every day from the fields to feed to cows that were outwintered. It was simply a matter of pulling them from the ground, trimming off the roots and soil with a shawing knife and throwing them onto the trailer. That's easier said than done on a frosty morning when they had to be chapped out with a heavy hammer. After that the cows often waited till midday for them to thaw enough to eat. Often they rolled them down the hill till they ended up at the back of a dyke.

We also fattened sheep on neeps by fencing off a small part of the field that provided about four days grazing to reduce waste. Snag with a frosty spell was that you couldn't drive the fence posts into the frozen ground. Worse, the lambs could only eat the leaves, as the neeps were too hard to gnaw.

The main problems with frost start when it turns into a spell of really hard penetrating frost. Apart from the horrible chill first thing in the morning after leaving the warm kitchen, there's also the problem of getting tractors to start.

After feeding the stock the next task is often defrosting the water pipes in the cattle sheds. When there's frost about I always drain those pipes in the early evening, so I only have to defrost the taps and inlet pipes. Sometimes the pipes freeze in the afternoon before I can drain them and that can be a real headache.

Thawing such pipes involves standing on an old milk churn to reach them in the eaves. Pouring cups of hot water on the pipes above your head ends up with half of it running down your sleeves or dripping off the pipes on to your head and down the back of your neck.

Pipe joints get forced apart by the expanding ice and trying to join them with numb fingers often results in the tiny copper rings being dropped and lost in the muck.

I remember in the winter of 1995 it became very cold during the day and the entire plumbing system froze in the main cattle shed. It has about two hundred and forty feet of pipes making it impossible to thaw with hot water, so I had to cart water to the cattle.

Every day, for about a week, my wife and I filled up ten 5-gallon plastic containers with water from a sink at the back scullery of the farmhouse. Then I ferried them round by tractor to the cattle sheds and filled up the troughs. Giving them all a daily drink took us about five hours so we spent all of that Christmas Day feeding and watering cattle.

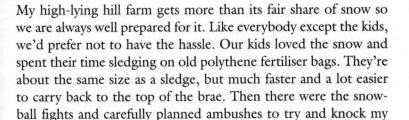

My high-lying hill farm gets more than its fair share of snow so we are always well prepared for it. Like everybody except the kids, we'd prefer not to have the hassle. Our kids loved the snow and spent their time sledging on old polythene fertiliser bags. They're about the same size as a sledge, but much faster and a lot easier to carry back to the top of the brae. Then there were the snowball fights and carefully planned ambushes to try and knock my bonnet off. While it's grand to see youngsters having fun, snow can make things on the farm a bit inconvenient.

Often the first thing to go in a blizzard is the electricity supply. Towns and villages get priority over farms when it comes to restoring supplies. Engineers also have problems checking our remote power lines.

Experience has taught us to have a good supply of gas-burning lanterns, the type used by campers, as well as torch batteries and candles. We have also learned to use brass candlestick holders that are far safer than saucers or wine bottles.

Heating is never a problem as we have plenty of coal and logs for the living-room fire and the kitchen is kept snug by our oil-fired Rayburn cooker. That Rayburn also heats our water and lets us have piping hot meals during a power cut.

Food reserves are a priority on a remote hill farm, for us as well as the animals. Our two freezers are well stocked with bread, meat, vegetables and home baking and my wife keeps the larder full at that time of year.

Biggest problems can be caused by snow drifting on our steep farm road, often cutting us off from the outside world. Even a light covering of snow makes it impassable to all but tractors and Land Rovers. Kids always enjoy time off school and it's nice when the postman can't deliver those bills, but it's always a worry that if anything goes wrong it's hard to get help.

I sometimes spend an afternoon clearing away the snow with the tractor foreloader. Moving tractors around the farm buildings can also be impossible until the snow has been shoved to the side.

The road can also become dangerous with packed snow and ice and it becomes nearly impossible to reverse the tractor and feed trailer up the slippery slight inclines to the cattle shed, straw shed and silage pit. To overcome those hazards I always have a small stock of salted road grit.

Outside on the farm is seldom a problem as sheep are good at finding shelter and feeding themselves. They scrape through the snow to nibble at grass and heather shoots. Sometimes as they do that, small pieces of snow roll downhill forming snowballs. Even if the snow freezes hard, they can last a long time without food, although I wouldn't let them starve. I always have a big enough stockpile of hay and feed, but there's no joy in digging through snowdrifts to get a tractor and trailer loaded with hay to the hill.

It's also a bit of a task carrying bales through snow and hard work digging out snowbound sheep, but none of these jobs are impossible. Our worst experience with drifting snow occurred after a blizzard in the late winter of 2001 when scores of sheep were missing and stuck in snowdrifts. I eventually found and dug most of them out, but despite that I had to bury six.

Four had got stuck in a snowbound burn and drowned, while the other two had suffocated in a compacted drift. The rest of the flock were OK but such events take their toll on heavily pregnant ewes.

Every snow-covered field tells an incredible story of activity. There are hundreds of scrapings from grazing sheep and foot-prints everywhere. Thousands of tracks made by rabbits and hares criss-cross every field.

Hares tend to lie up during the day in the thick cover of rough hill land. At night they move down to the fields to graze, as field pasture is sweeter and more nutritious than that on the hill. Following those hare tracks, you often see the narrow single line of fox tracks. I rarely see foxes on this farm but, judging by the number of tracks they leave, I'm overrun by a plague of them. Or maybe it's just a couple of foxes fruitlessly criss-crossing the fields in the hope of finding something to eat.

It's amazing the things a fox gets up to in the course of a night. Their tracks go right through the farmyard within feet of the backdoor. Then they circle the hen houses as they check all the doors are properly shut.

Most foxes get by on a diet of voles, worms and the like, but a significant proportion take the easy option and kill poultry, game birds and young lambs. Some occasionally kill purely for pleasure and I have seen a hundred and fifty hens killed in a night of carnage.

Foxes don't often kill healthy lambs. Those that are taken were probably weak or abandoned. Often foxes are simply a lame excuse for bad shepherding.

It's only natural that a hunter like a fox should take easy prey to feed its den of cubs, but I have known foxes to mutilate grown sheep. Sadly foxes attack sheep whilst they are stuck, or couped as we say, helplessly on their back.

I am against fox-hunting by horse and hounds, but I have to say that foxes need to be humanely controlled. Increased afforestation and fewer gamekeepers have seen their numbers rise dramatically.

Some naturalists argue that when fox numbers become too great in relation to the supply of voles or rabbits, they fail to breed successfully. That may be so in some cases, but it's when food becomes scarce that some turn to poultry and lambs. After all, it's their basic instinct for survival that has made them so successful.

Although foxes are happy to venture out when it's snowing, my best advice is to stay indoors when the worst of a blizzard is raging, as there's always plenty of time to sort things out in the calm after the storm. It seems a misery at the time, until you remember that every passing day brings us a day nearer spring.

The west of Scotland bears the brunt of the Atlantic storms and is the windiest place in Europe. So torrential rain and gales don't take us by surprise, particularly on this exposed hill farm. My wife comes under severe pressure in a prolonged wet spell. By ten o'clock in the morning, the Rayburn cooker becomes surr-ounded with sodden coats drying out. Wet scarves, gloves and bonnets cover the top of the Rayburn, as well as wellingtons packed with newspaper. Draped over its front rail are jeans, boiler suits and woolly sweaters.

Because it's impossible to dry washing outside, the pulley that hangs from the kitchen ceiling is constantly loaded with dripping clothes. Everywhere you look, there are clotheshorses and chairs round every radiator.

I suppose to the untrained nose of a townie, the smell of a damp, farm coat, steaming next to the Rayburn, is overpowering. Even I have to admit that a farm wellington drying out is hardly pleasant.

Another problem with cold wet weather is that I suffer badly from chapped hands and gegs. Those little cracks at the corner of your fingernails can be irritatingly sore. No matter how often I rub hand cream on my hands those gegs persist until the return of warm, dry weather.

Flooding is probably the biggest headache of all, with low-lying farms worst affected. Swollen rivers bursting their banks and flooding fields put grazing cattle and sheep at risk from drowning. Often as not, the beasts are saved by the farmer and his wife herding them on to higher ground by torchlight in the pitch dark of a stormy night.

Those who are caught out by an unexpected deluge face an even more unpleasant task, as they then have to coax and cajole stock, trapped on new-made islands, into fording waist-deep water in order to reach dry land. Sadly, not all such animals are saved.

Elsewhere torrents of water carrying leaves and other debris block farmyard drains, flooding cattle sheds, barns and other buildings. Clearing up the silty mess afterwards is another unpleasant chore.

Then there's the damage to farm roads as tons of hardcore are scoured out by rushing water and washed away. My steep farm road is about a mile long and particularly prone to such damage. At intervals along its length I have dug in heavy wooden battens at angles to catch surface water and run it off into the roadside ditch. But leaves and silt soon block those run-offs. End result is several days of hard work resurfacing the road, patching up the worst gullies with fresh hardcore and cleaning out run-offs and side ditches.

Ploughed land and fields of autumn-sown crops are particularly vulnerable. As streams and rivers appear from nowhere, thousands of tons of soil are washed away leaving behind deep channels and gorges.

There's nothing worse than a stormy night with the wind whistling and howling around the house, rattling the widows and forcing rainwater in along with the draughts. Doors banging in the wind, groaning trees or a loose sheet of corrugated iron rattling in the wind prevent even the most tired from falling asleep.

I have had many sleepless nights listening to the clattering and banging outside as skylight windows are blown in, or gutters and slates blow away. I have even seen pieces of heavy sandstone ridging torn off the farmhouse roof.

Sometimes we miraculously escape without any damage but more often than not a stormy night leaves expensive repair bills behind it. Everywhere trees are blown onto fences and roads and often the main culprits are old trees. That often happens after a really wet spell when tree roots haven't as strong a grip. Far too many old trees are badly in need of pruning or felling.

It's strange how we MOT cars, but ignore trees until they come crashing down. Despite that, I like trees, particularly in the autumn when their leaves change colour. They offer shelter and shade to farm animals.

Nuts like beech, hazel and acorn, or berries like rowan, are an important food supply for wildlife. Then there is all the insect life that feeds on their leaves or bark. Deciduous or broad-leaved trees are like fast-food restaurants. They're also safe refuges for all kinds of creatures that nest or roost in their branches, hide under their roots or live in holes in their trunks. It doesn't take many broad-leafed trees to make a farm an interesting place for wildlife.

Trees sway in the wind causing their roots to flex and heave the ground, toppling nearby dykes. It can take days to sort fences damaged by fallen trees or to clear away blocked roads.

Mind you, at the end of the day there's the bonus of a pile of logs to burn. My favourites are birch and ash as they burn well when freshly cut and even better when dried out. Beech and sycamore are also good burning but must be thoroughly dried first. Best burning is dry oak and hawthorn, though I seldom have them in my woodshed.

I have only once burnt Scots pine that burned fairly well and gave off a lovely aroma. My wife hates larch because it sends out showers of sparks that burn wee holes in her carpet. To avoid that she uses a spark guard that blocks the heat from the fire. Larch is commonly used for fencing and is best used as kindling. Mind you, if you want to shiver all night, cut up an elm. Freshly cut, or wet as we call it, it just sits in the grate smouldering and turning black.

Most folks nowadays have central heating and don't know how pleasant it is to spend a winter's evening sitting by a log fire. Of course, in years gone by a true hill farmer would have sat by a fire of peat. It gives a lovely glowing heat, with a grand smell and it burns away to nothing. If only we could rely on good summers to dry those peats!

11

All the fun of the fair

Farmers live and breathe their job and are only interested in farming. Socialising at a party or dance, we seek out other farmers. Huddled together in a corner we pass the night chatting about prices, yields or breeding policies.

Unlike townies, we find it difficult to talk about golf, theatre, foreign holidays or scandal. A night spent in the company of non-farmers is regarded by most as dull. That may make us sound boring, but if farming is in your blood, it fills your whole life.

It's often difficult during such social chattering not to be afflicted by a glazed, wooden look; a sure giveaway that we're bored to death.

To avoid embarrassment, we always try to turn conversations round to farming. After a while, you can usually observe the non-farming types in the group taking on a similar glazed look. So it's no wonder farmers feel most at home in the company of other sons of the soil.

Once we're too old to play football or rugby, few of us have other hobbies. Some enjoy a day's shooting, not so much for the pleasure of shooting game, but because it gives us a chance to inspect other farms. Many are the times I have watched pheasants safely fly unnoticed over a couple of farmers as they talk about the state of the crop they're standing in.

Truth to tell, many of us can no longer afford to shoot.

Instead we rent the sporting rights to affluent town folk. Others are conservation-minded and prefer to see pheasants strutting about their farm.

Quite a few farmers breed pedigree livestock or bring out show animals for a hobby. There's the fun of taking them round the various shows as well as selling them at a pedigree sale. Not to mention attending auctions and dispersal sales in search of that special purchase.

One hobby that can justifiably be claimed to belong to farmers is curling. As we are all self-employed, we can arrange to have time off during the day if we wish.

A rink of curlers comprises the skip and three other players. Four players is a comfy car-load, so another advantage of curling is that four of you can have a good farming blether as you drive to and from the ice rink.

A lot of farmers start to curl when they join a young farmer's club and over the years many of Scotland's top curlers have been farmers. I have only curled once in my life and I hated the game! Most of the afternoon was spent frantically brushing ice in front, or away from, the curling stone while the skip roared at us to brush faster. As I said to my wife afterwards, 'I don't like sweeping up when I'm working on the farm, so I am damned if I will sweep up for a hobby!'

For most of us, a day out involves going to the market or an agricultural show. Some of us are members of breed societies or management discussion groups like the Grassland Society.

Such groups organise farm walks during the summer and they are popular with farmers. Not only do we get the chance to chat, we also get to look round other people's farms. As with shows, such events only happen during the summer. Who wants to tramp round a sodden farm on a dreich winter's day?

During the winter we have evening meetings and annual general meetings. January and February tend to be packed with such meetings as, due to the weather, they are generally the quietest months of the year for most of us. Mind you, it's still amazing how often the chairman's wife will phone to say her husband is going to be late as there's a cow calving, tractor broken down, or whatever.

Held in local hotels or agricultural colleges, such meetings may take the form of a talk, backed by slides, by a leading geneticist, economist or nutritionist. After the usual pint at the bar, the organisers break up the little cliques and drag us through to the meeting hall. Warm stuffy rooms and the effects of that pint usually have some of us nodding off after a long day's work.

It's amazing how few speakers realise farmers aren't all that interested in how many mega joules or kilo calories there are in a cattle ration. Most of us simply feed a bit more if our stock isn't thriving. We are a body of men who often make financial decisions on the basis of calculations on the back of a fag packet. As a result, complicated lectures from economists don't turn us on either as we leave all that to the accountants.

As Cha is always quick to enquire, 'if they know so much about it, why aren't they farming themselves?' His other favourite question is to ask the difference between a banker and a terrorist. After a moment's silence he replies that at least you can negotiate with a terrorist!

Best part of the evening is the discussion after the main speech. That's our chance! There are always a couple of awkward old so-and-sos at the back of the room. 'That's not practical', or 'we can't afford that' are the sort of comments that have us all nodding in agreement.

I remember my father once caused a ruckus at a meeting where the principal speaker bemoaned the plight of dairy farmers. 'I will believe you lot are hard up when I see you having to cycle to your curling', he mischievously quipped.

At another meeting, a notoriously, long-winded speaker advised 'we'll all end up with egg on our faces when the shit hits the fan!' That statement is still regularly repeated today by those of us who heard it first.

Eventually the meeting breaks up for a cup of tea and the chance to return to our cliques to blether about farming again.

After the turn of the year is a favourite time for farming conferences. They tend to be organised by big companies or organisations seeking to raise their profile in the industry and are often attended by parliamentary dignitaries. If a spin-off comes in the way of increased business for the promoters, so much the better for them.

Held in fancy hotels and conference centres, these gatherings cost the earth and very few farmers attend them. There may be hundreds of people in the audience, but I will bet there's hardly a callused hand among them. Watch them buy a round of drinks and you won't see any binder twine, oil-stained hankies or penknives laid on the bar as they search their pockets for change.

Real farmers can't afford such events. More importantly, they can't get away for the two or three days they last. Farmers are stuck in the milking parlour, cattle yard or lambing shed coping with the industry's problems rather than discussing them.

They aren't missing much. I have been to a couple of conferences and I have to say that I found them boring. After the main speeches there was always a long-winded, irrelevant question from some self-opinionated windbag. Later, at the bar, there were bankers, lawyers, accountants, lecturers and politicians all talking about golf, theatre, foreign holidays and city scandal. Obviously not real farmers!

A good outing is the AGM of the National Farmers Union of Scotland that is usually held towards the end of February. Each area of Scotland takes its turn to host the AGM and I remember attending one year when that duty fell to Fife and Kinross, who had to provide the food for the dinner. Dunblane Hydro was the venue that year and over four hundred of us gathered to discuss our problems and elect our leaders.

Great care and pride is taken in using only food grown in the host's own area. Everything for the meal, from the meat to the fruit, fish to vegetables, oatcakes to whisky, was from Fife and Kinross. A starter of pork terrine was followed by a fish course from the fishing villages of the East Neuk of Fife.

After a raspberry sorbet there were fillets of chicken breast with mushrooms-in-whisky sauce accompanied by some of the finest vegetables I have ever tasted. That was followed by a sweet of rhubarb tart and custard, followed by locally made cheese and oatcakes. It was grand to enjoy such a spectacular feast and even better to watch the others.

Within five minutes of sitting down in the warm dining room, most had taken off their jackets and rolled up their sleeves.

One burly farmer next to me complained that it hadn't been much of a meal. I explained the sorbet was only a refresher halfway through the meal and not the sweet at the end. He hadn't realised we still had the main course to come! 'Ower muckle fancy', he grumbled. 'We wad hae done better with a bowl of broth and a plate of mince and tatties!' There's no pleasing some!

Next morning, after a massive breakfast, we went to the conference hall to listen to a speech from John Major. All that morning security had been very strict in the hotel and as the PM's arrival drew near, security became tighter.

Several times an announcement was made for the owners of unaccounted cars to report to reception, warning that if they failed to do so within ten minutes the police would tow the car away. Twice I watched farmers, who hadn't a clue what their registration number was, debate whether the vehicle in question was theirs.

Those incidents speak volumes about what farmers really think of their cars. Perhaps if the receptionist had described the vehicle as having straw in the back seat or that the boot smelled of pigs, she might have got a quicker response.

Looking at John Major's slim figure as he delivered his speech, I couldn't help think the PM needed a few dinners like the previous night's to fill him out.

Unlike John Major, sheep and cattle are greedy and constantly on the lookout for hay, silage and concentrated feed, even though that isn't natural. Their natural diet is grass and we have to train them to eat man-made foodstuffs like cake. It's a mixture of protein sources like soya beans and rapeseed meal as well as energy-rich cereal by-products, such as maize gluten or brewer's dried grains. It comes in a pellet form we call cake.

Most learn fairly quickly, but some never eat from a trough. That's quite rare in cattle but not uncommon in sheep and hill breeds can be the worst to train. There's nothing more frustrating than a non-feeder standing aloof while the rest tuck in to their daily rations. Invariably she will give birth to small, weak lambs. Worse, in a bad spring, she will be too lean and won't produce enough milk to rear a lamb properly.

The best time to train farm animals to eat out of a trough is when they are young. It's amazing how quickly a young lamb learns to mimic its mother and nibble beside her at the morning feed.

I always used to train replacement ewe lambs to eat out of troughs in the autumn. Sadly, I am often too busy and before I know it, it's the beginning of October and they have to head off to the lowland farm for the winter.

It's important that they are trained, so that when a snowstorm or prolonged bad weather comes along, we can quickly boost their rations. For a number of years I have been trough training the gimmers, or young ewes, at the turn of the year. They're about twenty months old and in lamb for the first time.

Idea is to run them in a small field that's short of grass. Obviously they learn a lot quicker if they're peckish. Another trick is to run a score of older ewes in the bunch to show them what it's all about. Every morning I sprinkle a little feed into the troughs, round the sheep up and keep them huddled round the troughs for ten minutes or so.

After a fortnight, I walk off those that won't feed while the rest are busy guzzling. Those delinquent so-and-sos are then penned in a very small paddock for a further week. Finally, the last non-feeders are caught and put in a shed for a week. That has the advantage of keeping them very close to the feed troughs and hayracks.

Our mule gimmers usually learn within a week to ten days as most of them have experienced feed when they were young lambs.

Before I start to feed the sheep, in or around the middle of February, I always draw off the leaner ewes so they can be fed separately. Feeding time for a batch of a hundred sheep is a case of the survival of the fittest. Weaker ewes are shoved aside and don't get their fair share.

Idea is to start feeding all the ewes about a fifth of a kilo per head per day and gradually increase their daily allowance until it's at its maximum of about three-quarters of a kilo per sheep every morning, about a fortnight before they lamb. Those ewes that suckle twins are often fed for a further six weeks after lambing until the grass is growing vigorously. That's why farmers are always so keen for an early, warm spring. Sheep cake costs about £140 a ton and my flock can guzzle about £400 worth a week.

Once I have laid out the lines of troughs I then have to round up each lot of sheep with my dogs. Though sheep are greedy and will knock you over to get at their feed, they also have very small brains and short memories. So every winter, when you call them up to the troughs for the first time they assume you are going to dip or dose them and run away. Once the dogs bring them nearer to the troughs they smell the cake and greedily rush forward.

Next morning the dogs aren't needed because each lot will be patiently waiting at the troughs. Then it becomes a daily contest to see how quick and nimble I am. It's bedlam! Like trying to walk against the flow of a football crowd.

Feeding sheep often involves a lot of skill and fancy footwork. If you aren't quick enough off the mark, a hundred hungry ewes soon engulf you. Often they take the feet from under you, and you suffer the humiliation of being trampled into the mud.

It's the mud that makes things so difficult. Sheep have four small hooves, one at each corner of their body and that makes them stable and sure-footed. Man on the other hand slithers about on two long legs stuck into a pair of slippery wellingtons. So every time you try to sprint to the troughs with the feed bag, you slip in the mud and are overwhelmed.

Mind you, though sheep may have agility on their side, farmers are more cunning. My secret weapon is to use my wife as a decoy. The strategy involves her approaching one end of the long line of troughs and, as the sheep charge towards her, I start pouring feed at the other end.

Crafty sheep will never starve and learn lots of tricks to get a little extra feed. When feeding a large flock of sheep I often lay out several bags of feed beside the line of troughs. The sheep soon learn to nuzzle open the bags for a few hasty nibbles before I start to feed them.

Gamekeepers feed their pheasants from suspended self-feed hoppers filled with wheat. Pheasants learn to peck a metal plate or tongue at the bottom that trips a mechanism releasing small amounts of grain. I once had a group of ewes that learned to reach through the fence and gorge themselves at a pheasant feeder hanging in the wood. They simply kept knocking the mechanism with their noses until they had a big enough pile to scoff.

I often scan my ewes before I start to feed them, although it all depends on the winter. We get a specialist contractor in to give them an ultrasonic scan, just like at the ante-natal clinic at a hospital, and find out how many lambs each one is going to have. Ewes are best scanned from about the end of January until mid-February, so if it is a harsh winter I start feeding before that.

We set up pens in the straw shed so the contractor's expensive electronic equipment is under cover and near a power point. The ewes are individually caught and gently held by the neck in a special catching-crate. Then a handpiece that emits an ultrasonic beam of sound is moved over the ewe's tummy. The echoes are picked up by the handpiece and converted into pictures on a monitor. And they are pure magic!

You can actually see the skeletons of the little unborn lambs as well as their tiny hearts beating. The ewes can then be separated into groups depending on how many lambs they are going to have.

As the expert shouts out the number of lambs the ewe is carrying, Big Tam sprays a distinctive patch of colour on the back of its head. The preferred colour code is no mark at all for one lamb, blue for two and red for those that aren't pregnant, or eild as we say.

I remember the banter between Cha and Tam the first time we scanned. As we all got used to identifying the individual skeletons and hearts Cha would occasionally quip that he had just spied a good pair of ewe lambs or that such and such a single would turn out to be a plain-looking wether. Tam finally twigged that the equipment wasn't that good and that Cha was pulling his leg.

It is a real help being able to see all those unborn lambs in the womb. Knowing whether a ewe is eild, carrying a single, twins or triplets allows us to feed more accurately.

In the past, some of us fed all ewes as if they were carrying twins. As a result, those that only had a single lamb received too much and ended up having difficulty giving birth, often to a big, dead lamb. Other farmers fed as if the entire flock was only going to have singles and drew off leaner ewes for preferential treatment. That saved on feed bills, but twins from lean ewes tend to be weakly and often perish in cold, wet weather.

Apart from saving feed and being able to keep ewes at the correct body condition, there are other advantages from scanning. Multiple births need more supervision, so those with twins or triplets can be kept in sheltered fields near the farm buildings.

Best of all, scanning saves the shepherd's legs. It was a weary-ing job walking twins from the lambing field to the fields where lambed ewes were nursing. Then of course, those with singles had to be walked to the hill gate.

Nowadays, all the singles lamb in the field next to the hill. Twins and triplets are lambed next to the pastures they will end up rearing their lambs in. I reckon that saves me about ten miles a day of walking sheep to, from and through various fields.

One of the drawbacks of scanning is that it highlights the mortality rate. Some lambs will never be born, as their ewes may die or miscarry. Others are stillborn or die shortly after birth from hypothermia. Disease, accidents and predators also take their toll. As a rule of thumb, I expect to lose about 10 per cent of all lambs scanned.

It's one of the sad truths of farming that the number of lambs we produce can have little bearing on our final profit. In years with good lambings there is often a glut of lambs on the market and prices are depressed. You shouldn't count your chickens before they are hatched or, in the case of sheep, sell your lambs before they are born.

I well remember a telling comment made by the scanning contractor to Cha one year. 'We are the last of our kind. This way of life is dying out'. Suddenly it dawned on me that we are all at least middle-aged and there are certainly less of us. Imperceptibly, over the years hundreds of shepherds, farmworkers and farmers have disappeared.

At one time, a flock, or hirsel, of 450 ewes was big enough to cover a shepherd's wage and leave a decent profit. Now it has to be at least 1,000 with the aid of quad bikes.

Trees have displaced sheep on vast tracts of Scotland. Elsewhere, sheep numbers are being reduced or removed altogether to encour-age heather regeneration to develop grouse shooting or deer stalking. Trees and grouse may be more profitable, but they don't need the same labour.

Shepherd's cottages are now holiday homes. Village shops,

schools and post offices close and a way of life is disappearing forever.

One of the last social gatherings for shepherds is the local herd's fair that is held towards the end of February. It used to be held at Candlemass (2 February) and was the largest of three annual fairs held in our town.

On that day, the street was filled with strapping, stalwart men clad in home-made clothes, the black-and-white plaid being universally worn, either folded carefully over the shoulder or draped round the body. Each carried a stylish stick with a long stock and had his collie at his heels.

The herd's fair was a hiring fair and after the men had struck their bargain with the farmers for another term of employment they held a great celebration in the town, though even in drink it is said they were calm and civil. The same could not be said for their dogs, and much worrying and fighting took place, though little damage ever seems to have been done.

By the end of the nineteenth century the fair had become an annual gathering to sort out lost sheep. Those strays they couldn't find homes for were sold and the proceeds given to the local poor.

Nowadays the fair is but a shadow of its former self, as shepherds become an endangered species. It is now held in a large hotel and starts about mid-morning. All morning the town is full of strange cars as shepherd's wives from far and wide drop off their men for their annual get-together and binge. The day now revolves round a carpet-bowling tournament held in the function hall of the hotel, with trophies for both pairs and singles.

Shepherds don't get out much, because they tend to live in isolated places. So when they do come down from the hills, they know how to enjoy themselves. For some it will be the first time they have seen their herding pals since the cast-tup sales or even the autumn sales and the crack at the bars is always fast and good.

Despite the hotel laying on big plates of piping hot stovies for bar lunches, the standard of bowling deteriorates as the day progresses and there are often tales of herds kneeling to bowl, never to rise again. All too soon, closing time is heralded by the arrival of a flotilla of cars driven by tight-lipped wives. Shepherds are hunted for, scolded and packed into cars to be driven home in silent disgrace.

Next morning, many rue the folly of the previous day, or do they? Remember that's their last big fling for some time. As the workload builds up to the hectic lambing season, there will be no time for nights on the tiles. Rising at five in the morning, walking the hills and working with sheep till darkness leaves a man too tired to even think about a night out.

I remember a shepherd asking Cha what was best for a hang-over. Without any hesitation he replied, 'take plenty of drink the night before!'

12

From little acorns . . .

When I first took the farm my cows mostly calved in the autumn. Because that works against nature, it tends to be a more expensive system. Cows that are suckling calves during the winter months need expensive concentrated feed to make up their diet. Cows that calve in the spring on the other hand can be weaned in the autumn, and as they aren't suckling a calf during the winter can be fed a cheaper diet based on home-grown fodder. Cows that calve in the spring milk well at grass and because they are rapidly gaining weight are also easier to get back in calve. Like most hill farmers I now calve my cows in spring and early summer.

The master plan is to calve about half the herd indoors in February and early March, lamb the ewes in April and early May and then calve the rest of the cows at grass in late May and early June. Sadly, as Tam loves to quote, 'the best-laid schemes o' mice an' men gang aft agley' and I often end up calving and lambing at the same time.

When cows are calved indoors it is so much easier than out in the fields because everything is at your fingertips. If a cow needs assistance I simply walk into her pen, restrain her with a halter and assist her. If I am not sure a calf has had that vital first feed of colostrum, I halter the cow again and persuade the calf to suckle.

Calves that are slightly off-colour are easily caught and injected with antibiotics and, when a young calf is poorly, it's no problem putting it into a deep-strawed pen and hanging a heater lamp overhead to keep it warm.

As the main cattle sheds are only yards from the farmhouse checking the cows is no hassle, but outside in the fields or on the hill it's a different kettle of fish. It can be very difficult finding cows at night, even with a torch. When you find a cow needing help, you may not be able to catch her so she has to be walked all the way back to the sheds. That's the problem outside. Every time something goes wrong, the animal has to be brought in to the sheds to be caught and treated.

Spotting sick calves isn't so easy either, as the little blighters lie low in the rushes, thistles or nettles and are almost impossible to find. My favourite trick is to mimic the sound of a calf calling for its mother. Often that's enough to encourage the cow to run to where she left her youngster.

It doesn't always work, as cows don't always know where their calf is. Many are the times an anxious cow and me have both criss-crossed the hill searching for a lost calf. Usually they're sound asleep and perfectly OK, but you can never be sure.

Unfortunately I don't have enough room in the sheds to calve all my cows indoors, as cows with young calves need a lot of extra space. So the best I can manage is to calve about half the herd inside.

Things can get hectic when there is an overlap and cows are calving at the same time that ewes are lambing. No sooner have I got round them all, than it's time to start again. I finish work most nights in April at around 9 p.m., have a wash and go straight to bed. The alarm is set for 5.30 a.m. and I like to be in the cattle sheds before six.

The secret to lasting the pace is to get a good night's sleep and that's hard at that time of year. Cows often calve during the night. Normally I put them into individual, straw-bedded pens as they approach calving. That's not always possible if there are a lot of cows calving at the same time and cows can calve sooner than expected.

Newly born calves run the risk of being trampled in the main cowshed, so once a cow has started to calve, she should be moved to an individual calving pen immediately.

Luckily I am a light sleeper and usually hear the distinctive lowing sound they make when they are in labour and the unique blend of bellows just after the calf is born. Then it's simply a matter of getting out of bed for fifteen or twenty minutes and moving the cow to allow her to calve in comfort.

There is something miserable about getting out of a warm bed in the middle of the night. Everything always seems so cold and dark out in the steading but, torch in hand, I always go out to see what is going on.

That system worked well until I fitted double-glazed windows in the farmhouse. My wife reckoned that was a big improvement on the old draughty windows that also let in dust and rain.

Unfortunately I could no longer hear my cattle through the double-glazing so I started to get up regularly through the night to check them. There's nothing worse than needlessly losing precious sleep so I came up with a solution that doesn't please my wife. I now leave our bedroom window open at that time of year so I can hear the cows as I used to.

It's not uncommon for cows to calve prematurely and such calves are usually stillborn. I remember one such calf that was very premature and particularly small, being less than a third of the normal size. The cow was standing in the corner of the pen, licking the lifeless little form and nudging it with her nose to try and wake it up.

Judging by the shortness of the calf's hair and the fact it hadn't formed any teeth I guessed it was about two months premature. As I went to lift it out of the pen one of its forelegs moved slightly and I realised the wee mite was alive.

The best chance of survival for a weak, premature calf is to keep it warm. Just as premature babies are put into incubators at the maternity clinic, I concocted a similar set-up. I made a small pen out of four bales and lined it like a nest with warm, dry straw. Then I hung an infrared lamp above it, and whilst it wasn't as posh as a proper incubator, it was just as effective.

Then I put the wee calf in a wheelbarrow and the cow followed me down into the yard with motherly concern, her nose never more than a few feet from the barrow.

After a couple of hours my wee friend was able to sit with his head up. The next problem was to give him a feed of that vital first milk or colostrum. It's very special milk that the cow produces for a few days after calving. Not only does it start the calf's stomach working properly it also contains valuable antibodies that protect it from many of the farm's bugs.

The snag was, having calved prematurely, his mum's udder hadn't formed properly, but after a struggle I managed to draw a couple of pints off of her. It was obvious the wee calf wasn't strong enough to suckle and pouring milk down a weak calf's throat is dangerous, as some of it could get into its lungs and damage them. The answer in such cases is to use a stomach tube. It's a plastic pipe about the thickness of your pinkie with a blunt end. Gently passed down the calf's throat it allows you to pour milk straight into its tummy.

Young calves need a lot of colostrum in the first twenty-four hours to ensure a healthy start to life. Luckily a dairy farmer friend gave me a gallon from a cow that had freshly calved. Small regular feeds soon had the wee calf on his feet.

Next problem was to train him to suckle. As he was still too weak to stand and feed from his mum, I trained him using a whisky bottle with a rubber teat attached. By the end of the third day I had him back with his mother and suckling normally. He grew out to be a fine beast. 'From little acorns mighty oak trees grow.'

Mind you, not all calves are as easy to train to suckle as that one. You often get big dopey calves that lie about, rather than make the effort to get onto their feet and suckle. Others are born to cows with large pendulous udders with teats that hang so low that the calf can't find them. There are also cows with teats so large that a calf can't get its mouth round them and others with blind teats that contain no milk, causing the calf to lose heart.

First thing is to restrain the cow with a rope halter and, while my wife holds the cow's tail to stop it being flicked into my face, I try to get the calf into position to suckle.

Some won't stand properly and keep lying down, while others stubbornly raise their nose high in the air and refuse to have it pushed down to the level of the teat. When you do get the calf into the correct position, you have to put the teat in its mouth and squeeze some milk out to let it get a taste. Often as not, they stand there sullenly and let the milk run out of their mouth, occasionally with a gurgling, choking sound. Eventually the cow becomes restless and kicks you on the shins or swings her backend round and knocks you into the muck.

Another frustrating trick is when the cow kicks the calf just as it starts to suckle. That's often because the teats are tender because they are swollen with milk. It can take a lot of patience and a bit of courage to work with a kicking cow and a timid calf.

Having been regularly kicked and trampled over the years I have to say that the stomach tube was one of man's finest inventions. A combination of that and a whisky bottle fitted with a rubber teat is often an easier way of getting colostrum quickly into a way-ward calf.

Calving time can have pleasant moments as well as disappointments. I remember a morning when I couldn't find the mother of a calf that had been born during the night. Sometimes newborn calves stumble through the feed barrier as they learn to stand. They then totter along the central feed passage, with its row of pens on either side of it, and crawl into another pen of cows. That's not uncommon and isn't hard to sort out, as a fresh-calved cow is easily spotted.

A simple way of finding the pen that contains mum is to walk the calf along the feed passage because mum will be the one anxiously bellowing for her calf.

Anyway, that morning there was a little red bull-calf standing forlornly in the passageway. Further along, a freshly calved cow was licking a newborn, black bull-calf in the corner of her pen. Try as I might, I couldn't spot the mother of that wee red calf.

Eventually I went into each pen to find the other cow that had calved. A cow that is close to calving has her calf lying on the right-hand side of her tummy.

Pushing your knuckles gently but firmly into the right side of her tummy swings the calf away. If you then keep your hand firmly in place you will feel the calf's head swing back against your knuckles. I checked every cow that was due to calve to confirm that she hadn't already done so.

Eventually it dawned on me that I was dealing with a pair of twin calves. The cow that had calved had given birth to a red calf as well as a black one. The red one had fallen through the feed barrier leaving his black brother behind with mum. Once I was absolutely certain, I put the cow and her odd twins into a pen by themselves. Sure enough, she fussed over both with equal concern.

Identical twins are probably as rare in cattle as in humans. I have heard of cows having different breeds of twins and on several occasions I have seen ewes give birth to twin lambs that were different breeds after being served by different sires. Nothing is ever straightforward with farm animals!

Twins aren't all that common in cows and probably no more than about 2 per cent of my cows have them. That's just as well, as more things can go wrong with twins and it's common for one, or both, to be born dead. As they're smaller than normal calves they're also more prone to disease in the early stages.

A common problem with twins is being presented in the birth canal in what we call the breech position. That's where they arrive backwards, tail and bottom first, with back legs tucked firmly under their tummy. It is almost impossible for a cow to calve a breech presentation unassisted, so I often have to fetch a bucket of water, soap and a towel.

I gently push the calf's bottom back into the womb and extend one of its hind legs so that it is pointing backwards. Once both hind legs are fully extended, a gentle pull soon has the calf out.

Calves that have been born backwards sometimes ingest birth fluids into their lungs and that causes them to have difficulty breathing. In such situations I lift the calf onto a gate so that it hangs upside down. A couple of hearty slaps on its chest clears away the suffocating mucous from its throat and lungs. Then I lay them on the ground and gently poke a piece of straw up their nostril. When the straw touches the delicate membranes in the nose it creates a reflex action that starts them breathing. Modern resuscitators are all right but they're never handy when you need them. You can always find a bit of straw, though, and it's the oldest trick in the book!

There is nothing more rewarding in farming than watching a calf revive after such elementary procedures. To see the cow licking the calf as it lifts its head from the straw is always a magic moment for me and puts me in a good mood for some time after.

Sometimes a heifer calf is twin to a bull and there is a high risk that the heifer is a freemartin. That's where hormones from her brother in the womb could have impaired her development internally. Freemartin heifers have a high chance of being non-breeders. To remind me not to keep them for breeding I always give them a special ear-tag.

It's always good to have a cow suckling twins as a spare calf comes in handy to foster onto a cow that has lost hers. I used to buy in spare calves from a dealer but stopped that many years ago as it introduced disease to the herd. I would rather let a cow run without a calf than run the risks associated with buying one in.

Often as not there is always a spare calf being suckled by an old cow I wish to cull or, with luck, a pair of twins.

Most cows are kindly, and as long as you drape the skin of her dead calf over the one you are fostering, they will invariably accept it as her own. Unfortunately, a fair number of foster calves refuse to accept such cows as their new mum.

That happened in the case of the little red bull-calf twin. About three weeks after those unusual twins were born a cow lost her calf. It had suffocated as a result of part of the birth membrane being draped over its nose and mouth.

Suspecting that the little red bull-calf might be reluctant to accept a change of mothers, I penned it by itself for twenty-four hours, to make it hungry enough to want to suckle. All through the night the wee calf bawled out for its mother whilst its mother roared back from another shed. To make matters worse, the dogs realised something was wrong and barked all night as well.

Next day, I fitted the skin from the dead calf over the little red bull and took him to meet his new mum. You might have thought he would have been glad to have a cow all to himself, particularly as his black brother had become quicker off the mark and was suckling more than his fair share. Not a bit of it!

You will have heard the saying that you can lead a horse to water but you can't make it drink. Well this was something similar. The only difference was the wee calf would struggle and wriggle free. Then I had to try and catch the wee rascal as he jouked about the pen. Fortunately, hunger finally got the better of him and he finally relented and suckled his new mum. Once started, he greedily made up for lost time as he twigged it was better to have a cow all to himself.

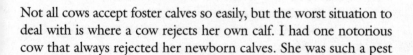

Not all cows accept foster calves so easily, but the worst situation to deal with is where a cow rejects her own calf. I had one notorious cow that always rejected her newborn calves. She was such a pest that I eventually culled her for that reason. Whenever she calved all hell would break loose. Roaring and bellowing at the calf, she would keep butting it every time it tried to stand. That's not uncommon with freshly calved cows, though most soon settle down after a few minutes. Experience had taught me that this cow would persist in butting her calf until she either injured or killed it.

As soon as she started her aggression, I would pull her calf away and put it into the next pen. That way she could see and smell her calf through the gate whilst being prevented from hurting it. Once she had calmed down and started to make those gentle lowing signs that a caring cow makes towards her calf, I would restrain her with a rope halter and give her calf a suck of colostrum.

Invariably, I had to stand with that awkward cuss three times a day for nearly a week to allow her calf to suckle without being kicked. It was always a relief when she relented and allowed her calf to suckle, but not as big a relief as the day I loaded her onto a lorry and sent her to market. As Cha often says, 'we have enough problems with the good ones without having to keep bad ones'.

Working with livestock is always interesting and you would be amazed at some of the strange things farm animals get up to. Like when a young calf swapped mothers, something I have never seen before.

It had been born to an older cow with a badly shaped udder, and I had trained it to suckle her by lowering its head almost to the ground. Eventually he started to regularly suckle all the milk in her udder and that helped to raise it higher off the ground. With her pend-ulous udder and massive teats, that cow was certainly no show stopper, although it has to be said that she was a good milker and that was the reason she had got into such a state over the years.

I check the calved cows twice a day and on several occasions I spied that calf stealing milk from other cows by suckling them from behind while they were suckling their own offspring.

That's a common enough trick with greedy calves, so I thought little of it until I noticed his mother's udder had become swollen with milk. Suspecting her udder had become so tender that she was kicking her calf away from her I brought them into a wee field near the house for closer observation.

Later that day I heard the calf roaring for its mother as if he had lost her, only to find her patiently standing beside her noisy calf. Incredibly, he was roaring for the cow he had been stealing milk from and not for his real mum. He had rejected his mother and adopted another cow with an udder that was easier to suckle. So I had to take that cow and calf back into the shed and persuade him to suckle his mother again. Hunger is the best tutor in such matters and he once again accepted his mother and forgot about his adopted one. Despite that, I never trusted him again and they spent the rest of the summer away from other cows in isolation in a wee field at the back of the house.

When cattle start to calve they become restless and lift their tail slightly. If they're outside, they go away by themselves to a sheltered and secluded spot. Indoors, they also manage to keep apart from the rest of the beasts in the pen, or rather, the other beasts know to give a calving cow extra room. From that stage, until finally calving, can take up to twelve hours though most complete the process in three or four.

A calf being born normally comes head first, with both forelegs stretched out in front of its head, so the first thing you see is a couple of front hooves. Sometimes a front leg is pointing backwards, other times both legs will be back and only the head is in the birth canal. Calves also come backwards and occasionally in the breech position I described earlier. There are other variations on these, but generally they are relatively easy to sort out. The one type of calving most cattlemen dread involves really big calves. You can often tell by its feet and the thickness of its legs if it is a big calf and that assistance is badly needed. Fortunately this is simply given by using a calving jack. It's a ratchet-type device that firmly pulls two ropes attached to the calf's forelegs.

Assisting a calving cow requires patience. Rushing the job or applying too much pressure at the wrong time will hurt her. The idea is to slowly ease a big calf out one click of the ratchet at a time. Once their shoulders are clear they often suddenly plop out with a rush.

Sometimes the bones in the hip of a big calf get stuck in the pelvis of the cow and that can damage the nerves to the cow's back legs. That can lead to temporary paralysis of the back legs so that the cow can't stand. It can take several weeks of nursing before such cows recover and some never do and have to be put down. Other times the calving is so long and protracted that the calf dies in the process. Big calves are truly a nightmare!

One of the biggest calves ever to be born on this farm was delivered by Caesarean section recently. It was a monstrous Beef Shorthorn cross-bull-calf whilst its mother was a little Aberdeen Angus cross heifer calving for the first time.

It happened in June when the cows were out at grass and I had been observing her all morning. By lunchtime she was no further forward and had rejoined the rest of the cattle so I brought her into the sheds for an examination. Although the calf was coming normally, it had rather large feet, so I phoned the vet. He suggested leaving her for another hour and then to ring him back if she had made no progress.

The vet was finally summoned after lunch when it was obvious the beast needed assistance, and it didn't take him long to work out that the calf was too big for a natural birth.

Fortunately it was a quiet beast. The vet shaved the hair from her left side and then injected her with local anaesthetic and sedatives. As she became drowsy we pushed her on to her side and then prepared the cattle shed like an operating theatre. A junior vet was summoned to help while we laid plastic sheets on the straw bedding, set up an old table and laid out all the surgical instruments on it.

Those two vets made it all look so easy. They opened up the heifer and then lifted the big calf out of its womb. As one vet revived the newborn calf the other one held on to the womb in preparation for stitching it up.

The whole operation took about half an hour and at the end of it we had that heifer on her feet and admiring her newborn calf. Next task was to draw off some colostrum and feed it to the calf, as we didn't want it suckling the heifer, as her belly would become painful as the anaesthetic wore off.

Next morning I let the calf in beside its mother and steadied her as he suckled. Every morning for the next five days I injected her with antibiotics to prevent the wound from becoming infected and she eventually made a full recovery.

I am always keen to learn the sex of all newborn calves. Bull calves grow faster than heifers, end up a lot heavier and attract special European subsidies. In other words, bull calves are worth more than heifers and are usually more profitable. As soon as a calf is born, I nip into the pen and lift its back leg to see if it is a bull or a heifer. Quite often the cow will give me a fright and threaten to charge. Suckler cows can be very protective of newborn calves and resent people interfering with them.

They paw the ground with their front hooves and shake their head to warn you that it is time to clear off. I always take the hint and quickly retreat to a safe distance because suckler cows can be every bit as dangerous as a bull.

That point isn't always understood by town folk as they go for walks in the countryside. Little dogs, particularly when not on a lead, can enrage suckler cows to the point where they will charge both dog and owner.

Fortunately my cows are kindly and soon settle down and will happily allow me to fit ear-tags to their calves the next day.

According to the cattle-identification regulations, farmers must apply two ear-tags, one in each ear, to a beef calf within twenty days of its birth. We then fill in forms with the official ear-tag number, the sex of the calf, its breed, date of birth and the official ear number of both its mother and father. Those forms are used to apply for individual passports for each calf and that must be done within twenty-seven days of its birth. All the information is stored on a central computer at the British Cattle Movement Service (BCMS) and the passport must accompany the calf whenever it is sold or moved to another farm when all such movements are recorded. The system has been designed so that all cattle can be traced in the event of a disease outbreak.

At one time there was a degree of flexibility and late applications resulted in a warning not to be late with future applications, but new strict rules mean that all late applications are now rejected.

Passports are important because they entitle farmers to special subsidies. More importantly, because it is illegal to move cattle without one, they can't be sold and become worthless. It's important we get it right, as officials don't allow mistakes.

This paper chase depends on farmers being able to see clearly and read tags properly. Hence the reason I need my glasses when sorting out cattle and their passports for market. Fortunately, poor eyesight is my only disability unlike a friend who is dyslexic. After a visit by ministry officials concerned by the number of mistakes he was making, he now gets his wife to read those ear-tags and fill in the forms. Farmers are heavily penalised for making mistakes whilst officials seldom admit to making them.

If the BCMS computer was to be believed, I once had a miracle story to tell. According to it, one of my cows gave birth to a healthy calf despite having been dead for two years.

Cattle born before 1996 didn't have passports until November 2000. It was a lot of hassle and involved tedious form-filling as well as ear-tag reading, but eventually we received passports for those older cattle that had been born before the system was introduced. Snag was, there had been a gremlin at work and one of my cows was already recorded as having been slaughtered.

After lengthy correspondence, an official visited my farm and confirmed that the cow was alive and the beast that had been slaughtered must have had the wrong ear-tag number on its passport.

Sorting computer errors can be difficult. When that cow calved again the following year I applied for a passport for her calf and you can imagine my disbelief when the computer informed me its mother was still dead.

BCMS phone lines are constantly busy, but after a few days I eventually got through and was told that the easiest way to sort the problem was to re-tag the cow with a new number. Despite giving the cow a new identity it took months to get a passport for the cow and its calf. The computer would not accept our attempts to sort the problem, and stubbornly reckoned that a dead cow had given birth.

Now that really would have been a miracle!

SPRING

13

The best dog I ever owned

March is a month when the days are noticeably stretching out and there can be a feeling that spring is in the air. It's a time when snowdrops in the garden are fading as daffodils start to burst their buds.

Meanwhile the hill is once again alive with the sound of peewits and curlews that have returned from their winter quarters by the coast. Skylarks, too, are once again soaring into the sky to join in the chorus. There's nothing more uplifting than listening to moorland birds on a warm, spring morning. Mind you, I have lived long enough to know that, 'March can come in like a lamb and roar out like a lion'.

Towards the end of March I bring the ewes into the pens to give them their annual booster vaccination. Sheep are prone to all kinds of illnesses, including clostridial diseases that often cause sudden death. About a fortnight before lambing, I give them an injection that will protect them against eight different diseases. Another benefit is that newborn lambs also become immune by suckling the antibodies in their mother's first milk or colostrum.

Mind you, nothing is ever straightforward with sheep. I keep them confined in batches of a dozen in a long narrow pen we call a dozing race. Then I part each sheep's fleece at the side of its neck and lift a fold of skin so that I can inject it just below the skin.

Once, just as I was about to do that to a ewe, she jumped on top of the ewe in front. In the commotion I accidentally injected the index finger on my left hand that was holding the fold of skin. Needless to say, the air was blue with my oaths at the pain. That left me with a sore finger for some time as well as wondering if I was also immune to eight different sheep diseases!

Once the ewes are vaccinated I then organise my lambing shed in a twenty metres by eleven metres straw-shed that has to be cleared first. That means that I have to find alternative accommodation for about ten tons of straw. Then a winter's accumulation of bits and pieces – machinery under repair and the like – has also to be tidied away.

Finally, fifty individual lambing pens are erected in two double rows. I make them out of industrial packing-case-sides that I bought from a local factory for a few pence each. Then the lamb adopters have to be set up. These are individual stalls that secure ewes whilst an additional orphan lamb is being fostered on.

Lamb warming-boxes and old barrels with heater lamps suspended above them have to be wired up ready for reviving lambs suffering from hypothermia.

Then there's all the other paraphernalia of lambing time that has to be assembled. Medicines like iodine and antibiotics, syringes and needles, lubricants, ointments, marker sprays and the like in case of emergency.

Finally I hang a wee blackboard in front of each pen so that I can chalk the day and time of admission, what the ewe is in for and what medication she has received. That's a big help now that I am becoming more forgetful when under pressure. Better still, it allows my wife to see what has already been done when I am away in the lambing fields.

Good collie dogs are the tools of my trade and it is impossible to lamb sheep without one. While you can never have too many, you should have at least two to share the heavy workload. A third, or 'spare dog', is also essential, because inevitably one will either hurt itself or go sick when you are at your busiest. I try to have a minimum of three dogs, two fully trained and a young one coming on. I never keep bitches because they cause so much trouble when they come into heat.

At one time it was relatively easy to buy a trained collie as most shepherds kept three or four and always had a litter of pups as well. Young dogs were trained, and then sold, for badly needed extra cash.

A top dog nowadays will set you back over £3,000 whilst poorer ones, or pot lickers as they are called, fetch about £1,000. Anyway, price isn't the only issue as they are now almost impossible to find and most adverts attract dozens of phone calls. I prefer to buy pups and train them myself.

Many people think that there is a mystique attached to training sheepdogs, but nothing could be further from the truth. The secret is to win the dog's respect and become friends. After that he will always respect you as the top dog, the leader of the pack, and will spend the rest of his life trying to please you.

Sheepdogs work naturally and, even as puppies, will try to round up chickens or ducks. All you have to do is patiently encourage the right things, and discourage the wrong.

Essentially you teach a sheepdog to stop and lie down, to come towards his sheep on command, to go to his left and go to his right. With these four basic commands, a genuine affection between dog and man and the animal's natural desire to work with sheep, anybody can train a sheepdog.

My training regime begins with me teaching the dog his left from his right. 'Come by' is clockwise and 'away to me' is anti-clockwise. Fifteen minutes of repetitively calling 'come by' or 'away to me' is one of his first daily lessons. Then he has to be taught to lie down on command and wait patiently for his next command.

That's not an easy task for a keen, young dog. Once he knows right from left, and can be stopped, he is then taught all the other jobs like driving sheep away from you or separating out sheep from the main flock.

I have had the good fortune to work some fabulous dogs in my life. Whilst it is true that you can't teach an old dog new tricks you would be amazed how quickly a young dog will learn the tricks of his trade.

Although it's always nice to have an experienced dog at your heels I have to say that a big hill lambing is a young dog's game. Apart from the stamina needed to run vast distances every day, a dog must have plenty of power in reserve. He could be called on to outrun and catch a ewe or lamb that needs treatment.

When a dog goes to catch a ewe, he steadily closes in on her, wearing her down with his eyes. Sheepdogs can stare intensely at a ewe until she simply stands quivering, allowing the shepherd to catch her. Other times the sheep will make a run for it. On comm-and, the dog will run alongside, grip the wool round her neck with his teeth and literally pull her to the ground. Such feats require strength and speed.

Many dogs that I have owned over the years have learned to catch young lambs. When given the command to catch the lamb, they run alongside it and trip it up by turning their nose in front of it. After two or three tumbles the lamb usually lies down.

The best dog I ever owned was called Max, and had been bought as a household pet by a friend who lives in a nearby town. He was 'ringle-eyed': that's where one eye is normal but the other has a white iris round the pupil.

As with all collies, Max was an active dog bred for a life out of doors. His exuberant trick of jumping onto the settee to greet the postman, or standing on his hind legs with his paws on the window sill to bark at passing cars, did not endear him to the mistress of the house. Particularly when those antics led to ornaments getting knocked over and broken. I bought him from his exasperated owner for £40 and trained him to be a sheepdog. He soon learned his trade and became equally good at working with cattle.

His favourite pastime on the way to work was to pick up large stones in his mouth and drop them at my feet. I would then kick them as hard as I could while he chased after them and fetched them back. Perhaps his best trick was finding lost lambs. On the command 'Meh! Meh! Where's the lambie?' Max would hunt through rushes and heather till it was found and then stand barking over it.

I accidentally ran him over with the Land Rover although, fortunately, he died instantly and suffered no pain. He was supposed to be in retirement after ten years of hard work, but that wasn't his style. Every morning when he heard the back door of the farmhouse open he would wander round to greet me with wagging tail. No way was he going to let me head off to the lambing fields without him.

After I had loaded up the Land Rover with bags of feeding, he would hop in the back with my other two dogs Bob and Roy. There he sat as usual peering out of the widow over my right shoulder. Whenever Bob, Roy and I got out to catch a ewe, Max would jump out to watch the proceedings. It was almost as if he didn't trust us to do the job properly on our own. You could clearly see his disapproval if we made a mistake.

Newly-lambed ewes can be very protective of their young. Often they will chase a dog to butt him. Max had his share of spills and tumbles and preferred to keep out of the way. So, when a ewe was being brought into the sheds in the back of the Land Rover, he preferred to trot alongside rather than risk being butted on his arthritic hips.

The morning of the accident we were bringing a ewe and her twin lambs in for attention. As usual, Max was making his own way back but he never arrived at the shed. That wasn't uncommon. As master of his own routine, he often took time out to investigate unusual smells, sounds or sights.

Being hard of hearing, he often temporarily lost track of where we were. But, knowing every nook and cranny of the farm and my work routine, he soon sussed out where I was and followed on. So I wasn't concerned as I retraced my steps to pick him up, only to find him dead on the track. I had unwittingly run him over as he cut across the path of the Land Rover.

He died the way he would have wanted. Working in a lambing field on a beautiful spring morning was a far better ending for Max than lying about the yard. He can never be replaced and I will always have fond memories of him.

I am sure his spirit lives on. I regularly get the feeling that he's watching, as usual, as we go about our work in the lambing fields.

Not all dogs are like Max. Attacks by Rottweilers and pit bull terriers made headline news that forced the government to pass legislation controlling dangerous dogs. It's a sad fact that most dogs, not just the more aggressive breeds, are capable of turning nasty. I remember a hound that escaped from a hunting pack in the Lake District and roamed far and wide. Despite all efforts to catch and destroy it, it killed and maimed a large number of sheep.

That highlights the fact that most dogs are potential killers. Despite my sheepdogs being properly trained, gentle and affectionate I still don't completely trust them. When they're not out working or having supervised exercise, they're kept locked in their secure doghouses. Even at tea breaks or meal times, they're never allowed to lie about the yard untended. They are always taken back to their quarters and shut in. Only old, trustworthy dogs in retirement are allowed the freedom of the yard.

Some of the worst sheep worriers can be collies, particularly young, half-trained dogs that are eager to work. Given half a chance, they will head off looking for sheep to round up. Without the steadying influence of their master, a situation can soon get out of hand and sheep are injured or killed.

Although sheep worrying doesn't receive much publicity, it's a major problem in farming. Many farms on the outskirts of towns have been forced to abandon keeping sheep because of it. Packs of half-wild stray dogs chasing pregnant ewes at lambing time can do untold damage. Losses are not always limited to the dead sheep. There are those that are maimed or miscarry their lambs.

Even the most affectionate family pet can be a danger. It annoys me to see folk who are out for a picnic allowing their dogs to roam loose, as they should always be kept on a lead.

Dogs running wild can soon disappear. After much shouting they usually return panting, but what were they up to in those ten or fifteen minutes they were missing? Were they playfully chasing rabbits, or worrying sheep?

Strange dogs frighten sheep, and the sight of one can have them running in blind panic. Young lambs trying to follow their ewes can fall into ditches or streams and drown. They may even run in the opposite direction of their mother and get lost. Panicked sheep may get caught up in briers.

Without actually biting or chasing a sheep, the most affectionate family pet can inadvertently harm them. I remember the local police once tracked down a mad killer that had been on the rampage in the district. A big black mongrel had moved in with strangers who had taken up residence nearby. It was often seen running loose and unattended, and was suspected of a spate of sheep-worrying incidents that had happened since its arrival in the district.

The first incident happened at a neighbouring farm where a pregnant ewe had its ears chewed off and its legs badly bitten. Then it was the turn of my sheep. One of them, a pregnant gimmer or maiden ewe, and scanned as carrying twins, was found badly mauled. She also had had her ears chewed off.

Worse, she had vicious bites on the back legs and her chest had been badly mauled. The dog had been powerful enough to get its jaws round the gimmer's brisket and had punctured the rib cage with its teeth.

I phoned the police and called for the vet, who put the distressed sheep to sleep. Sadly the injuries were too severe, and there was no point in letting the gimmer suffer needlessly.

Although I gave a full description of the dog to the police, there was nothing they could do until it was caught in the act. That happened later that week when another neighbour found it attacking some of his sheep. That allowed the police to approach the owners and insist that the dog be destroyed. Such action may seem drastic, but once a dog becomes a killer, there's no cure.

If only the poor creature had been properly supervised to start with, it might never have turned to its cruel killing ways, and cruel they were. In addition to the gimmer that was savaged, another five ewes miscarried dead lambs as a result of being chased whilst heavily pregnant.

Ever since I started farming I have had a car and a Land Rover, which may seem a luxury, but I can assure you it isn't. Living on an isolated farm, it's vital to have a reliable working vehicle because when help is needed quickly, transport is vital. Thankfully such crises rarely happen, but two vehicles are essential. Children have to be taken to and from school buses. At the same time, livestock may have to be taken to market or spare parts collected urgently.

A Land Rover is an ideal second motor for a farmer. Not only can it negotiate our steep farm road in the worst of conditions, it can also haul the livestock trailer.

Its main use is for feeding and checking stock. A sick ewe can easily be put in the back for a hurl to the steading. Many a lamb suffering from hypothermia owes its life to those minutes next to the heater as it's rushed to the lambing shed. Most of the essential medicines I need are kept in the Land Rover, so sick animals can be treated immediately. You could describe it as a paramedic's ambulance for farm animals.

Over the years, my dogs have learned to work sheep by commands given from the moving Land Rover. My top dog always sits in the back looking over my shoulder. When I want to round up sheep, I let him out of the back and give him the command. While he gathers one side of the field, I gather the other side by blowing the horn. I accept the system will never be seen on *One Man and His Dog*, but it's quick and saves the legs.

It is a feature of most lambings that you tend to get your problems at the start. Most lambings start with tiny, premature lambs, or weak triplets out of lean ewes. Often as not they are stillborn or die shortly after birth from hypothermia. Many are the times that I have found premature lambs lying flat out with hypothermia. In such cases I catch the ewe and put her into the back of the Land Rover for a quick hurl to the lambing shed whilst her lambs lie close to the heater in the front.

First task is to warm the lambs up, by putting them in an old barrel with straw in the bottom and an infrared heater-lamp suspended above it. I also use a lamb-warming box: that is, a wooden box with a perforated floor through which warm air from a thermostatically controlled convector heater is circulated. Both are equally effective although you have to regularly check lambs in the barrels in case they become too hot.

After tending to the lambs I then inject the ewe with a long-acting antibiotic as premature births are often caused by an infection. Then I draw off the colostrum into a bottle that I feed to the lambs by stomach tube as they begin to recover. It's a soft rubber tube – about the thickness of a Biro – that is passed down the lamb's throat and into its stomach in the same way as with a calf. The combined effect of heat and colostrum usually helps most lambs to fully recover within a few hours.

Next task is to train such lambs to suckle their mother. That is a bit like teaching granny how to sook eggs, as most take to it like a duck to water. Occasionally, as with calves, you get an awkward cuss that tries your patience and refuses to suckle at the first few attempts, but most of them learn within a day or so, and it is rare to lose a lamb that never learned.

As I said, it's not uncommon to find premature lambs lying dead. In such cases, I also catch the ewe, bring it into the lambing shed and inject it with antibiotics. I then milk her three times a day and store the milk in the freezer to be fed later to lambs with ewes that are short of milk. Within a few days there will always be a spare lamb to foster from ewes with triplets or those that have had twins but not enough milk to rear both.

Mother Nature only provides ewes with two teats, so rearing triplets isn't easy. There's always one poor lamb that has to wait patiently for supper. That often leads to the smallest one becoming a runt. To avoid that, I foster one of the triplets onto a ewe that has lost her lamb. Over the course of a lambing there are plenty of opportunities to foster surplus lambs and I rarely have any orphans, or pets as we call them, at the end of a lambing.

All pet lambs are bottle fed for a few days before being put in a straw-bedded pen with an automatic ewe. It's a bucket with four teats that allow them to suckle when they want. At the height of lambing there can be as many as a score of pets, but I always aim to have them all twinned by the end of lambing. While they do reasonably well on artificial milk for a few weeks, it's hard to rear them successfully to maturity.

Many die from bloat, a digestive disorder, while others die from intestinal parasites as a result of eating a lot of grass too early in life. Those that do survive become pests, not pets. Fearless of man and dog, they learn to raid the garden for flowers and vegetables. Those that are eventually sold never repay the costs and hard work involved.

The most important thing at lambing time is to ensure every ewe has at least one lamb. After feeding a ewe all winter, it would be silly not to have her nursing a lamb. Even sillier would be letting one lie idle while another struggled to nurse twins or triplets.

Sadly, about 15 per cent of all lambs die within forty-eight hours of birth. Some are born dead, others die from disease, but most die from hypothermia. It's amazing how quickly the wee mites perish in cold, wet weather.

Hunger plays a big part in hypothermia. Without a tummy full of milk, lambs just can't generate enough heat to keep warm. Some lambs don't learn to suckle quickly enough. Others can't because of the shape of the ewe's udder. Commonest problem, particularly where a ewe has two or three lambs, is simply a shortage of milk. It sometimes takes a day or two for milk production to start properly.

When a ewe hasn't enough colostrum of her own, we give her lambs some from another ewe or even cow colostrum. I also keep stockpiles in the freezer and, as a standby, I have a powdered substitute. In the old days shepherds used to mix milk with raw eggs, cod liver oil and glucose to make a substitute. Nowadays there are specially formulated powders that we mix with water.

I remember one morning my wife offered to make up some artificial colostrum for a pair of hungry lambs. After breakfast and a few hurried phone calls, I picked up the jug of creamy liquid she had left out for me and fed the lambs.

Imagine my horror when later on that day my wife asked me what had happened to the jug of Yorkshire-pudding mix she had left on the kitchen units. In my hurry I had lifted the wrong jug.

Although it didn't do the wee mites any harm, I wouldn't recommend it. Fortunately, the Yorkshire-pudding recipe is quite like the old shepherd's recipe for colostrum substitute.

In rough weather we do our best to get sheep to shelter but every year I revive scores of lambs that have succumbed to the cold. No matter how diligent the shepherd is, it's inevitable that lambs will die. Therefore one of the main chores at lambing time is fostering or 'twinning-on' lambs to ewes that have lost their lambs.

Initially, ewes identify their lambs by smell and as they get older they learn to recognise their bleat. As with a calf, the trick when twinning a lamb is to fool the ewe into thinking that the new lamb smells like her own. Often, we drape the skin from a dead lamb over the one we intend to twin. Mum sniffs the skin and accepts the orphan as her own. A few days later, the skin is removed and dumped.

Another way is to rub the orphan lamb in the ewe's birth fluids before they have been licked off a lamb. That's a good trick if there isn't a skin, such as when twinning an extra lamb onto a milky ewe that has just had a single. If you are too late, and the birth fluids have been licked off, there is always the lamb adopter.

It's a wooden, crate-like device where the ewe is restrained by putting her head in a yoke, rather like a wooden stock. That way they can't see or smell the lambs but can feel them suckling. After about twenty-four hours, once the lambs have picked up the same scent as the ewe, she accepts them.

One of the big problems at lambing can be with stealing ewes, particularly after a mild winter when they have more milk. With their udders swollen with milk they become desperate to nurse lambs. So, at the onset of labour, rather than wait for their own lambs to be born they seek out other lambs.

While a ewe is busy in labour with her second lamb, such ewes fuss over the first-born twin, and steal it away. I often find ewes with three or four lambs that have still to give birth! In such instances I isolate the stealing ewe in the sheep pens out of harm's way and then find the rightful owners of the stolen lambs.

Ewes that have had a lamb taken from them are easily spotted, but working out who owns which is harder. After being fussed over and licked by a stealing ewe, stolen lambs smell differently. As a result, some ewes won't accept their own lambs back and that can create a real problem. Once a ewe has made up her mind to reject a lamb she can be as stubborn as my wife!

Fostering-on lambs using a skin is easy, but getting a ewe to accept her own lamb after she has rejected it is virtually impossible. In such cases I try the lamb adopter and that often works, but not every time.

As a last resort I have used my wife's perfume. After sprinkling some on the ewe's muzzle I pour it over the back of both lambs. That fairly confuses her sense of smell and sometimes does the trick. Most times, though, the ewe wins and I have to twin the unwanted lamb onto another ewe, and face the music from my wife about wasting her perfume!

I remember an old ewe and a gimmer had twin lambs in the same corner of the field. I suspected the gimmer had lambed first, and the ewe – about to lamb – had been attracted to the noise of the newborn lambs bleating. Both would have fussed over the wee mites until the ewe lay down to lamb. Then it would be the gimmer's turn to assist in licking the next-born lambs.

Both ewes licking each other's lambs, as well as the lambs rubbing against each other, would soon have the smells completely mixed up. The end result was two anxious mums that didn't know which of the four lambs were theirs.

Fortunately it was easy for me to sort out. There were two small, dark lambs that obviously belonged to the wee gimmer, whilst the larger light-coloured pair belonged to the old ewe. Five minutes later I had the old ewe standing in one corner of the field with her twins and the gimmer with her pair in another corner.

At lunchtime, when I went round the field again, the old ewe was butting one of her lambs with her head. That's a ewe's way of rejecting a lamb that's not hers. The wee mite would stand bleating, the ewe would encourage it to run up to her by bleating back. Then she would sniff the lamb, decide that it wasn't hers and butt it away again.

Meanwhile the same was happening in the other corner as the gimmer was convinced one of her twins didn't belong to her. After swapping over the rejected lambs both the ewe and gimmer were content. Each was convinced it should have a large white lamb and a small dark one. It was obvious the sheep were wrong, but I was so fed up with their daft notions that I just let them get on with it!

Lambing is generally a rewarding and enjoyable task and it's grand to see a lamb take those first vital breaths after a difficult lambing. Sadly lambing has its disappointments as well, such as ewes that die despite being treated with the appropriate medicines.

There are times when I think a ewe's only ambition in life is to die. Anybody claiming they never lost a ewe at lambing time is probably fibbing. Those who declare they hardly lost a lamb are simply daft if they expect other shepherds to believe them.

Once buried, the casualties are soon forgotten and it's easy to think that only two or three have died. A quick tally often reveals that few lambings are without their share of misfortune. 'Never count your losses' is an old saying that is often quoted by farmers, because if you did you would become so depressed that you would give up.

There is a lot that can go wrong at lambing time. Apart from the vagaries of the weather, routine illnesses like milk fever and ewes needing help at lambing, there is a host of unexpected tragedies, like the time I assisted a ewe to have a large lamb.

First task was to catch her. Normally that's relatively easy, but this was a wild one that had to be hunted down by my two collies. After a difficult lambing most ewes stay with their lamb licking it and fussing over it, but not this one. She was so indignant at the way she had been handled that she bolted from her newborn lamb. Normally in such cases I catch the ewe again, tie her feet together and let her lie quietly with the lamb for quarter of an hour. If, at the end of that time, she's still showing no interest in the lamb I pen the pair together in the lambing shed.

As this one was in a decidedly uncooperative mood, I went to get the Land Rover to fetch her in. I returned to find that in her desperate attempts to free herself, she had rolled down a brae, fallen into a burn and drowned.

Then there was the time a couple of ewes with large teats needed to be brought into the lambing shed so that I could help their lambs to suckle. The first ewe was easily caught and put in the back of the Land Rover. As I loaded up the second ewe, the first one panicked, jumped over the back of the driver's seat and scrambled out of the open door. As I set off hotfoot with my dogs to catch her again, my wife followed behind in the Land Rover. Unfortunately, in the stramash, one of the lambs bolted in front of it and was run down. Such incidents are rare but can happen in the mad rush of lambing. But it's not all doom and gloom; I often end up with nearly a thousand lambs. As about one in ten are assisted in one way or another, that means I successfully save about a hundred lambs every year.

Such as the one that managed to climb up a thorn bush and then became suspended upside down by the hips caught in the fork of a branch! Like youngsters of all kinds, they do some daft things, and you need eyes in the back of your head at lambing time.

Occasionally we get ewes with a twisted womb where the lambs are trapped inside. A quick hurl to the vet for a Caesarean section solves the problem but the end result can be dead lambs and a sick ewe that takes days to recover. Often as not the vet's bill will be twice what the ewe is worth, but farming isn't just about economics. As I said, there is the satisfaction of saving a life.

Perhaps the most satisfying incident was when my wife saved a lamb being smothered by its mother. We were checking the lambing shed for the last time when I noticed a ewe lying on top of one of its lambs. I got that ewe on to her feet and handed the dead lamb to my wife to put in a polythene bag ready for burial. As she was about to dispose of it she noticed its heart was beating faintly, so she started to give it mouth-to-mouth resuscitation and heart massage. Incredibly, she got it breathing again. Next morning we had the pleasure of watching it head off happily with its twin sister and mother.

Jesus told a parable about the happiness of a shepherd on finding a lost sheep and I know how that biblical shepherd felt. Like the time a ewe lost one of her lambs down a rabbit hole.

I had helped that ewe to give birth in the grey light of dawn as she had been 'hanging' her lamb. That's where the lamb's head is protruding but both forelegs are folded backwards. Ewes can find it impossible to give birth when the lamb is stuck like that, but I managed to ease one leg forward through the pelvis and pulled a large black lamb away.

Her next lamb was white with a fawn-coloured head. I left that ewe fussing over her oddly matched pair. After breakfast I found her with the light-coloured lamb, whilst the big black one had been stolen by another ewe. I caught and lambed that stealing ewe and left her looking after her new twins.

When I returned the black lamb to its mum, she took one sniff and butted it away. After twenty-four hours in the lamb adopter she accepted that lamb and I released her into a small field for observation. Three hours later I found her frantically looking for the light-coloured lamb.

It's not uncommon for ewes to wander off leaving a sleeping lamb behind. A quick hunt round the field usually finds the dozy creature, but not this time and, after a thorough search of the adjacent fields, my wife and I concluded a fox must have taken the mite.

Later that day, I noticed movement in a rabbit hole that turned out to be the wriggling tail of a stuck lamb. As the Bible teaches, it's the lost sheep that's the most important.

———————————⌒

Foxes that attack livestock aren't all that common, but when one goes on the rampage it can be a real menace. Mostly Reynard does little harm as he and his vixen get by on a diet of voles, young rabbits, ground-nesting birds and carrion such as dead lambs. Occasionally, though, they kill live lambs, although often as not they are weak and dying. Sometimes a fox starts to take healthy lambs and there's nothing more exasperating than such a maverick.

Some say that a gamekeeper wiping out a vixen and her litter of cubs can start her mate on a trail of vengeance. Others reckon that when a hard winter kills off much of the fox's natural food supply they are forced to seek alternative prey. Whatever the reason, foxes do kill young lambs, and once started on such easy prey they are very unlikely to break the habit.

We once had such a dog fox in our area that killed more than fifty lambs one spring. His trademark was to chew the lamb's head and leave the rest of the carcass uneaten. That's unusual, so at first a stray dog or even a badger was also suspected. Eventually, farmers and shepherds spotted a big dog-fox killing lambs on several occasions.

Local gamekeepers organised a huge hunt for that fox. Forty farmers and keepers beat through all the surrounding fir plantations in the hope of flushing the killer into a line of waiting guns.

After two days of hard work they successfully drove that big fox out into the open. Either by luck or cunning he emerged in front of one of the worst shots in the district, who missed him with both barrels. So a great deal of valuable time and effort had gone to waste.

Alerted to danger, he became even more cunning and elusive and all sorts of measures were adopted to protect young lambs. Some farmers set up flashing lights in their fields to scare him away at night. Others patrolled their farms with Land Rovers and spotlights. One farmer walked all newly-lambed ewes away from the edges of the woods to the centre of his farm.

Ewes that had their lambs killed had to be caught and brought into the lambing sheds to have another lamb fostered on. Many complained that was almost impossible, as the fox had left his scent on the lamb as he killed it, and as a result most ewes rejected the foster lambs when they sniffed the skin. At £40 a time, that killer fox destroyed over £2,000-worth of lambs and created countless unproductive extra man-hours for keepers and shepherds at their busiest time of year.

The worst-affected farmer offered a bottle of whisky to the man who shot it. Despite umpteen bottles being handed over for smaller foxes that were shot, the real culprit remained at large. Eventually it was caught in a snare and we all breathed a sigh of relief.

Nature can seem cruel. All over the countryside, birds and animals are killing each other. Owls flit silently at dusk in search of mice and voles. Sparrowhawks and peregrine falcons patrol the daytime skies for other birds. Weasels and stoats stalk rabbits and small birds. Herons wade quietly in ponds and waterways searching for fish or frogs while thrushes and blackbirds greedily gorge themselves on insects and worms. There's little chance for weaklings or the unwary in the wild!

Despite the fact it's the most natural thing in the world for predators to kill and eat those smaller and less fortunate, it can be very frustrating at lambing time.

The main predators in the lambing fields are carrion crows, or corbies as we call them. Most of the time they do little harm, and feed on the carrion that's inevitably found in a lambing field. It's when they attack live lambs that I get very annoyed.

The corbies are only doing what comes naturally to them as scavengers that feed on afterbirths and dead or dying animals. The snag is, they don't realise a helpless, newborn lamb is perfectly healthy.

While a ewe lies down to have her second lamb, the corbies attack the first-born. Their vicious beaks soon peck out the eyes, tongue, navel and entrails. It all happens so quickly that, by the time I arrive on the scene, the lamb is in desperate need of being put out of its misery.

Carrion crows can wreak havoc in the lambing fields and some years I have had to put down a fair number of mutilated lambs. I wouldn't mind so much if the corbies killed the lamb and took their fill. After all, every creature has to eat, but they often only take eyes and tongues before moving on in search of another victim. I have even watched corbies hop along behind healthy twins that were following their ewe. After several vicious pecks the hindmost lamb would lie down and then be attacked.

I even have to destroy ewes that were attacked by corbies whilst couped, or stuck on their back. As they lie helplessly on their back with their feet pawing the air, those corbies will peck out both eyes and peck open their stomach near their udder.

Corbies have multiplied with the increase of forestry and because there are fewer gamekeepers around to keep their numbers in check. As a result, I now snare them with a Larsen trap. It's a cage about three square metres wide and two metres high. There's a hole in the mesh on top with a mesh funnel leading down close to the ground.

Dead rabbits are laid as bait and a couple of live corbies placed inside to act as decoys. They're fed and watered every day and attract other corbies to the trap that soon find the hole in the top and drop down the funnel to feed.

When they try to escape they haven't the sense to climb back up the funnel. Instead, they fly round the top of the cage looking for a way out. It's then simply a matter of putting them down humanely.

Interfering busybodies regularly release my decoys, rendering the trap useless. Presumably they wrongly assume that keeping decoys in a cage is cruel. If only they saw how much my sheep suffer they would soon realise the folly of their actions.

Sunshine is the magic ingredient in a successful lambing. Ideally there should be mild nights and sunny days so that the lambs are quickly onto their feet and suckling. Once they have filled their bellies with colostrum they lie down and sleep contentedly.

Within a couple of days they can run like hares. It's grand to see lambs playing and skipping while their ewes are feeding at the troughs in the morning. Usually they race off to a stone or knowe to play King of the Castle.

Folk tend to forget that sheep originate from the hot, arid climes of the Holy Land. Although generations of farmers have bred them to tolerate our dreich, wet climate they still prefer dry sunny weather.

Of course, even in fine weather, there are still problems. Commonest one is big lambs and ewes needing assistance at lambing as a result of extra grass growth in a fine spring. Instead of using the extra food to keep up their body weight, ewes also use it to give extra nourishment to their unborn lambs.

Although it's great to lamb in fine weather my memories are mostly of coarse, wet days when ewes and lambs take a battering in torrential rain.

Most ewes find a sheltered part of the field or hill, out of the blast, when they are about to lamb. The leeward side of a drystane dyke is the ewe's favourite, as it's almost as snug as being in a shed. Provided she isn't disturbed, she will stay there until the lambs have had several good suckles. When the lambs are several hours old she may start to graze again, but she'll never stray far from the dyke in case another sleety shower comes along.

Sadly, not all ewes are blessed with weather sense at lambing. Gimmers having their first lamb can give birth in some of the most exposed parts. Generally, when I see that happening in a rough spell I bring them into the lambing sheds until the lambs are at least twenty-four hours old.

In a really wet spell the fields become a sea of mud and impassable to the Land Rover. When that happens I hitch the transport box to the tractor. It's a cage-like device that can carry four ewes. All day long I ferry ewes and their newborn lambs into the sheds for shelter.

Eventually the sheds become stowed out with sheep, forcing me to start a rota system. The strongest go back out into the rain to make way for the weakest. Such a system may sound inadequate, but it's infinitely better than can be provided on a big, extensive hill farm that is managed traditionally. Often as not the ewes on such a farm can't be brought into sheds.

Hill farmers don't always feed their sheep during the winter. That's not because they can't afford to, but simply because such sheep aren't always accessible for daily feeding. Others believe that feeding concentrates produces a type of sheep dependent on feed and that flocks would lose their hardiness as a result.

Extensive hill systems work well until those years with a harsh winter and late spring. In extreme years many hill ewes become so lean at lambing time they don't produce enough milk. As a result, a fair number abandon their lambs. Cruel as it sounds, it is nature's way of ensuring the ewe survives. Even those that do nurse lambs are short of milk so that the lambs aren't well grown in the autumn. As I have said before, the weather plays a big part in farm profitability.

The secret of success at lambing time is to keep dry and warm as a wet and cold man is no use to anyone. Only the very best of waterproof clothing will do.

Another good tip in coarse weather is to eat well. 'It's the meat that does the work, not the man', is a true saying. Working hard in cold wet weather needs a big supply of energy, so a hearty breakfast, lunch and supper are the order of the day.

Finally there's the bath and bed. A good steep in a hot bath, followed by a wee dram, perks you up after a long hard day. Sleep is nature's great restorer and early risers must go to bed early. Nine o'clock at night is late enough when you're rising at five-thirty.

One of the worst lambings I ever experienced was in the

spring of 1994. After a long harsh winter that wore the ewes down, cold winds, heavy rain, sleet and snow took their toll.

Lambs never stood a chance and scores perished from hypothermia. My farm is very exposed and I expect to lose lambs in bad weather, but never on the scale I saw that year. Despite all the family putting in long hard hours, the weather finally beat us and left me with the worst lambing results of my life.

If there's such a thing as a bonus out of disasters like that, it was grand to see the family pulling together. My wife helped me feed the sheep and catch and transport those needing shelter. Back in the sheds the kids fed and watered the ewes in their individual pens and bottle-fed motherless lambs.

A taste of hard work did the youngsters no harm and the experience taught them that life is full of challenges and disappointments that have to be met head on.

14

Magic moments

There is an old joke about a farmer who wins the lottery and is asked what he intends to do with all the money. 'I'll continue farming until it's all gone', he solemnly replies.

Farming has never been an easy occupation. On top of all our difficulties, we have to cope with an increasing burden of paperwork.

VAT, PAYE and tax returns we have learned to accept. More recently we seem to spend more and more time in the farm office filling in ever more complicated forms; and they have to be completed properly, and on time, or we face huge financial penalties. There are movement records, risk assessments, subsidy claim-forms and a whole host of other forms that record every detail of our business.

On top of that hassle are routine spot-checks by officials that are extremely thorough and leave no stone unturned.

Farmers love to moan and complain about the weather, bad prices, form filling or whatever. Many of us have cried wolf so often that hardly anybody is prepared to listen when we are faced with real difficulties.

I am reminded of the tale of an undertaker who always buried farmers in shallow graves. The minister had noticed this and asked him about it. 'They like to be buried near the surface so they can still get their hand out', he replied.

I was once moaning to a non-farming friend about the weather and how I was overworked when he replied that I should give up farming and opt for an easier way of life. That certainly gave me food for thought.

How many folk would work long, hard hours for little or no reward? In those years when there are profits I have little cash to spend on luxuries. Any surplus is reinvested in better buildings or new equipment. Apart from an occasional day off during the summer to attend a show or wedding there have been few holidays. If I sold up tomorrow I would have little to show for a lifetime's work.

I farm for the way of life rather than the money. How can anyone put a value on a beautiful sunrise with the haunting cries of curlews on the hill? There are so many magic moments to be savoured, like a torrential April shower followed by the sun bursting through and the air filling with the sound of singing skylarks. Peewits diving and swooping low over collie dogs to protect their chicks or mystical hares boxing with each other.

A bank covered with delicate primroses, a wood carpeted with bluebells or the smell of honeysuckle in the evening are all pleasures that aren't easily bought. To watch a cow lick its newborn calf after helping her to give birth during the night is a feeling that's hard to value. Or the satisfaction of being told by other farmers at a market that your cattle are looking well.

Like most others, I would prefer to earn more money, but content myself that job satisfaction also counts for a lot. Going to bed tired after a long, hard day's work and sleeping soundly is another reward many of us take for granted.

One sure way of getting to sleep quickly at night is to spend a day lifting stones. As the days start to grow longer, particularly in March, ploughed land starts to dry out. Best conditions are when there's a dry wind blowing out of the east. 'A pickle March dust is worth its weight in gold.'

Stones have to be cleared away before the land can be worked into a seedbed, and I usually concentrate on the bigger ones that could damage machinery. Some folk break them up with fourteen-pound hammers, whilst others roll them on to a sack so that two or four men can lift them on to the trailer. I prefer to use the tractor fore-loader as I reckon you can't beat hydraulics for the really big brutes.

Some stones become well known to me over the years. Despite knowing roughly where they lie beneath the surface I always manage to hank them with the plough. Eventually they become dislodged and dragged to the surface and are often scored with countless grooves after generations of ploughs have scraped over them.

Once the stones have been removed and the land has dried out, it has to be disced. A heavy machine – comprising rows of massive saucer-like steel discs, mounted on axles – slices the furrows into rough clods. That also helps the soil to dry out quickly, particularly when an easterly wind is blowing. Then we harrow the land into a finer tilth by dragging a piece of chain mail mounted with steel spikes that is about four metres wide by two metres.

Once there's a firm seedbed of fine tilth, we sow the seed, harrow it again and roll it using a heavy roller that weighs about three tons. Such operations are relatively straightforward, though dull and monotonous. The biggest risk is missing a strip when sowing, so that your neighbours can laugh at your gaffe all summer.

There is often a cloud of dust following the tractor and you end up looking like a miner and ready for a bath.

Before rolling, there's still the backbreaking, leg-numbing task of lifting stones that could damage harvesting equipment. Despite generations of farmers gathering stones over the centuries, a fresh crop appears every year. There are so many that I am convinced stones are capable of reproducing!

At the start of the day, full of enthusiasm, you gather every stone bigger than a teapot. By lunchtime, when you're still only a third of the way across the field, you become less choosy. Anything smaller than a football is often left in the hope the roller will crush it back into the ground.

Come teatime, with legs aching after plodding all day over loose soil, most of us become very selective indeed. At that stage we're often driving the tractor and stone-laden trailer in ever-widening strips across the field. Instead of a strip that's twenty metres wide, we start taking in fifty metres at a time. That has the advantage of covering the field faster, as we don't spy stones that are lying further out.

Unfortunately, shortcuts seldom work. When you roll the field, guilt forces you to constantly stop and lift missed stones. Then they have to be transported to the edge of the field precariously balanced on the roller's drawbar, and a jolt can mean stopping for a second pick-up.

It's amazing how time flies when you are really busy and thankfully you find it's the middle of May and the mad, spring workload is nearly over. While cattle enjoy the warmth and comfort indoors during the winter storms they become restless in their sheds in May, as they yearn to be back outside at grass. They can smell the grass, feel the sun beating down on the roofs and know it's time they are outside.

They seem to know when the freedom to roam over fields or hill is imminent and start making more noise than usual. Every time I go near the sheds they roar and bellow. It's their way of reminding me in case I forget to turn them loose.

They, themselves, are reminded by the return of the chattering swallows that start renovating nests in the cattle sheds. There's also the dawn chorus of all the nesting birds in the surrounding woods, as well as the mournful cries of curlews on the hill at dusk. Finally, there are the balmy smells of summer as the rising sun lifts the morning dew, or when light rain falls on dry land.

The cows needn't worry, as I have also become weary of the

daily routine of feeding and bedding them, and start looking forward to having them outside at grass.

When I finally open the doors and gates, most of them charge off to the fields in a mad stampede. Having said that, there are always half-a-dozen young calves that temporarily suffer from agoraphobia. Born indoors in March, they have grown up thinking that a cattle shed is their natural environment.

They run up to the door eager to follow their mums and mates, but after a nervous sniff at the concrete yard they turn tail and stand cowering at the back of their pen. Eventually I drag the last few outside. After standing trembling for a few seconds, they take off, kicking their heels in the air in a mad, gleeful, headlong dash.

I remember disaster striking one spring, when a two-month-old calf ran up to a sleeping lamb to sniff it out of curiosity. Suddenly woken from its deep sleep, the lamb ran towards the calf thinking that it was its mother. That startled the calf and caused it to birl round. In a fit of exuberance rather than any malice, the calf playfully kicked its heels in the air and accidentally caught the lamb.

I arrived on the scene to find the wee mite with a broken back leg. Fortunately it was a clean break between the hock and the stifle and relatively easy to plaster. I simply cut up appropriate lengths of plaster bandage and steeped them in warm water. While my wife held the lamb's leg firmly in place, I applied those wet strips and waited for them to harden. The whole process takes about ten minutes at most.

After about ten days the leg was as good as new although, whilst it had its leg in plaster, that wee lamb kept a wary eye on those big cattle.

It's easy to forget why I wanted to be a farmer as I become embroiled in the day-to-day management of the farm. Rushing about trying to get seasonal work done on time or bad tempered due to being held up as a result of a breakdown or bad weather. Constantly striving to improve performance and yields in spite of disease, parasites, pests or bad weather. Worrying over unpaid bills or a soaring overdraft due to bad prices or crop failures after bad weather.

There is no doubt that the weather has a lot to do with a farmer's moods. It can have the biggest impact on farm profits and is completely outwith our control. A long dry spell, harsh winter or late spring can be very costly.

Politicians have tried for years to manipulate farm output by means of subsidies or production controls but, when all is said and done, it is Mother Nature who decides if there will be too much or too little.

A spell of fine weather always gets us all into a better mood. Crops and grass start growing vigorously, making up for lost time. Cattle and sheep love to have the sun on their backs. After a long winter or cold, late spring, an extra bit of warmth gets them thriving.

I love to walk round my stock in the evening after a sunny day. As cattle and sheep contentedly chew their cud I stop for a while and lean on my stick to admire them.

I am surrounded by some of the most beautiful and majestic scenery in Scotland. The air I breath is clean, and my way of life is healthier than most. All around there are peewits, curlew, soaring skylarks, hares and rabbits playing or relaxing. All enjoy the glorious gift of life on a summer evening.

That's why I am a farmer. It's not to make profits, or to worry and fret. I farm because it's all I ever wanted to do and because I enjoy it more than anything else.

I breed the next generation of livestock to be better, grow

heavier crops or improve the land not for money, but for the sheer love of doing a good job.

Obviously I have to make profits or I would soon fail, but profit isn't the main motive. If that was my only goal, there are easier ways to achieve it than farming. No matter how well paid, no job is worth doing if you don't enjoy it. A bunch of contented cows often remind me how lucky I am to be a farmer.

Spike Milligan once said, 'everyone gotta be somewhere', and the more I think about it, the more truth there is in that statement. If everyone has to be somewhere, then it follows that someone has to live on a hill farm like mine, a rented family farm with seventy beef cows and around five hundred ewes. In common with thousands of other farms, mine is now struggling to provide me with a reasonable living and things are unlikely to improve much in the foreseeable future.

Many times I have come home from market, scarcely able to believe the prices I have accepted, only to be more disappointed with the next sale. I once received a cheque for two pence after selling ten old blackface ewes and three small lambs that should have been sold at the autumn sales. Prices were so bad then that I didn't think I would get a bid for them, so I kept them in the hope that prices might improve.

Lamb prices did eventually increase by about £10 per head in early February, so I decided to sell them. Unfortunately, the trade slipped back again that day and they only fetched £1 apiece. After the auctioneer deducted £11.05 for his commission and £1.93 for VAT, I was sent a cheque for two pence. I framed that cheque and hung it on the wall above the lavatory as I believe such a bad trade is best put behind you!

I have also lived through the BSE crisis, the worst farming depression since the 1930s and the horror of the foot-and-mouth epidemic. Increasingly, I find myself muttering that my bleak farm is a land without hope. Then I remember what Spike said and accept that I am here instead of, say, Sudan where famine and death are real, and BSE and poor prices are not the main topic of conversation. Or I might have been born into a society suppressed by a homicidal maniac such as Pol Pot, ruling with threats of persecution, torture and sudden death. So, while I bemoan my lot and blame other people for my problems, things could be a lot worse.

Farming regularly goes through economic cycles and generations of farmers have had to cope and adapt. There's no doubt that while many farmers are suffering hardship, it's comparative. Few of us will go bankrupt or quit, as that's not our way. We will hang on and survive until times improve.

We don't have to do it that way. Many farmers struggling financially could sell-up, pay their debts and still have enough capital to retire. We are undoubtedly better off than a redundant farm worker who, having lived all his working life in a tied cottage with modest wages, has nothing to fall back on except skills that are no longer wanted.

Few farmers will suffer the real trauma of being made redundant and having to eke out the prime of their lives in misery, not to say poverty. Perhaps that is one of the reasons farmers tend to hang on at any cost. They realise that the alternative is too demeaning.

We know that life can be cruel and unfair. Some only live briefly while we all have to cry at some time. I believe that when it comes to personal tragedy, it's always got to be somebody's turn. We all lose people we love and ultimately face our own death. When real tragedy strikes, it puts farming's financial problems, all problems in fact, into perspective; no one can fix that for you.

The point is, that while it is right for us to argue our case vigorously and fight our corner, we shouldn't become too despondent when politicians can't, or won't, fix things.

Car manufacturers, steelworkers, shipbuilders, coal miners and textile workers have all seen their industries virtually disappear. Governments couldn't help. Perhaps that is where hill farming finds itself today? Perhaps we have to accept the inevitable and adjust to a new way of farming or of trying to cope with the future.

I enjoy being a farmer, have a roof over my head, I am well fed, live in a peaceful country and have a loving family. These may be small mercies, but three-quarters of the world's population would be glad to have them.